RELEASED

Reversing the Trend toward Early Retirement

Reversing the Trend toward Early Retirement

Robert L. Clark and David T. Barker

American Enterprise Institute for Public Policy Research
Washington and London

Robert L. Clark is an associate professor, Department of Economics, North Carolina State University at Raleigh. David T. Barker is an assistant professor of economics at George Fox College, Newberg, Oregon.

Library of Congress Cataloging in Publication Data

Clark, Robert Louis, 1949–
    Reversing the trend toward early retirement.

    (AEI studies ; 316)
    1. Retirement age—United States. I. Barker,
David T. II. Title. III. Series.
HD7106.U5C553   331.25′2   81-2313
ISBN 0-8447-3433-0   AACR2

AEI Studies 316

Printed in the United States of America

Contents

LIST OF TABLES

1

Public Expenditures on the Elderly and the Costs of Early Retirement

The growing cost of public and private transfers of income and goods to older persons retired from the labor force has stimulated considerable debate concerning retirement policy in the United States. These costs have risen because of an increase in the elderly population, the liberalization and expansion in coverage of transfer programs, and a decline in labor force participation of the elderly. In examining the trend in social insurance and welfare programs, former Secretary of Health, Education, and Welfare Joseph Califano, stated that federal expenditures for persons aged sixty-five and over have risen from $12.8 billion, or 2.5 percent of the gross national product (GNP), in 1960 to $112 billion, or 5.3 percent of the GNP, in 1978.[1] In addition, substantial benefits are available to older individuals before they reach age sixty-five.

The reduced market work of the elderly is both a result of benefit improvements and a cause of increased costs. Older persons withdrawing from the labor force decrease the number of taxpayers and increase the number of beneficiaries. This shift in work status raises the total cost of transfers to the elderly and also increases the proportion of income that those who remain in the labor force must pay in taxes to finance these benefit programs. The relationship between benefit programs, the retirement decision, and the total cost of transfers to the elderly is the principal topic of this study. The remainder of this chapter describes the growth and development of the benefit programs, examines the related rise in expenditures, and analyzes the

[1] Joseph Califano, "The Aging of America: Questions for the Four Generation Society," *The Annals of the American Academy of Political and Social Sciences*, vol. 438 (July 1978), p. 98. Also see, Robert J. Samuelson, "Busting the U.S. Budget: The Cost of an Aging America," *National Journal* (February 18, 1978), pp. 256-60.

increased public expenditures that would be necessitated by a continuation of the trend toward earlier retirement in the coming decades.

Transfer Programs Benefiting Older Persons

Since the 1930s the federal government has developed an extensive system of social insurance and welfare programs. The elderly have benefited directly from age-based eligibility programs as well as from programs designed to aid the low-income population. For those aged sixty-five and over, the principal transfer programs include Old-Age and Survivors Insurance (OASI), Disability Insurance (DI), and old age assistance (now Supplemental Security Income, or SSI), Medicare, and Medicaid. In addition, low-income elderly are eligible for in-kind benefits, such as food stamps and housing subsidies. Liberalization in these programs has contributed to the decline in the poverty rate—based on money income—of individuals sixty-five and over from 35.3 percent in 1959 to 14.0 percent in 1978. Data compiled by the U.S. Congressional Budget Office for fiscal 1976 illustrate the relationship between public transfer and proportion of the population aged sixty-five and older below the poverty level (see table 1). In 1976, the pretax, pretransfer poverty rate was 59.9 percent; the post-tax, post-total transfer rate was only 6.1 percent. The reduction in the poverty rate due to public policies indicated by these data probably overstates their actual effect because pretransfer income may be altered in the presence of welfare and retirement programs. Gifts from children may be reduced, and older persons may reallocate their time and resources in anticipation of public benefits.

TABLE 1

FAMILIES AGED SIXTY-FIVE AND OVER BELOW THE POVERTY LEVEL
UNDER ALTERNATIVE DEFINITIONS, FISCAL YEAR 1976

Income Definition	Families below Poverty Level	
	Number	Percentage
Pretax/pretransfer income	9,647,000	59.9
Pretax/post–social insurance income	3,459,000	21.5
Pretax/post–money transfer income	2,686,000	16.7
Pretax/post–money and in-kind transfer income	977,000	6.1
Post-tax/post–total transfer income	982,000	6.1

SOURCE: U.S. Congressional Budget Office, *Poverty Status of Families under Alternative Definitions*, Background Paper No. 17, rev. (1977), p. 12.

Because social security and other transfer programs provide income to the elderly, they would be expected to lower the likelihood that eligible persons will be in the labor force, and this will tend to lower the pretransfer income of the elderly. Many of the programs include earnings tests that reduce the gain from market work and thus may exacerbate the tendency to curtail hours of work. Also, during the last twenty-five years, social security retirement and disability benefits have been extended to people younger than sixty-five. Chapter 3 examines the available evidence concerning the effect of government transfer programs on a person's decision to withdraw from the labor force or to reduce his hours of work. Economic studies will be analyzed for findings on the primary determinants of retirement, especially those factors that influence early retirement, that is, retirement prior to age sixty-five.

Expenditures for Transfers to the Elderly

During the past two decades, aggregate and per capita public transfers to the elderly have risen substantially. Table 2 shows these significant increases in both the average benefit per older person and in total federal expenditures. The almost $100 billion increase in total ex-

TABLE 2
FEDERAL EXPENDITURES FOR PERSONS AGED SIXTY-FIVE AND OVER

Year	Average Expenditures per Person[a]	Average Expenditures Necessary to Maintain Real Expenditures in 1960 Dollars	Total Expenditures (billions)	Percentage of Gross National Product	Percentage of Federal Budget
1960	$ 768	$ 768	$ 12.8	2.5	13
1965	1,019	817	18.8	2.7	16
1970	1,902	1,007	38.2	3.9	19
1975	3,379	1,394	75.7	5.0	23
1978	4,678	1,648	112.0	5.3	24

[a] Expenditures per person are calculated by dividing total expenditures by the number of people aged sixty-five and over.
SOURCES: Joseph Califano, "The Aging of America: Questions for the Four Generation Society," The Annals of the American Academy of Political and Social Sciences, vol. 438 (July 1978), p. 98; unpublished Department of Health, Education, and Welfare data; and the authors' calculations.

penditures from 1960 to 1978 can be broken up into cost increases due to inflation, population growth, and benefit improvements. In the absence of improvements in real benefits and any growth in the number of persons over sixty-five, expenditures would have increased by almost $15 billion to reflect price increases during this period. Holding real benefits constant, expenditures would have risen by another $12 billion because of the increased number of older persons. The remaining $73 billion increase is attributable to the liberalization of benefit programs for the population aged sixty-five and over. This cost increase comes from the extended coverage of existing programs, increases in benefits per recipient, and the institution of new programs.[2]

Total spending on transfer programs is determined by interaction between the benefit level set by legislation and the individual response to the availability of transfer income. Higher benefits encourage more people to retire and accept benefits, thus raising total expenditures on the elderly. Considerable evidence documents the influence of the growth in benefits on the retirement decisions of individuals aged sixty-five and over. Less is known about the cost of retirement and disability benefits to individuals between the ages of forty-five and sixty-five and their labor-supply response to these benefits.

Retirement Age and the Cost of Old Age Transfers

The cost of providing income transfers to the older population is borne by the working population. To demonstrate the cost of early retirement, assume that everyone between the ages of eighteen and the fixed age of retirement is in the labor force, everyone over the age of retirement is out of the labor force and is eligible for retirement benefits. Then $TWL = BR$, or $TW = (R/L)B$, where $T =$ the tax rate on earnings, $W =$ earnings per worker, $L =$ number of workers, $B =$ benefit per retiree, and $R =$ number of retirees.

The tax per worker per dollar of retirement benefit is determined by dividing the number of beneficiaries by the number of labor force participants. If we use the 1978 civilian population, the implied tax per worker, as shown in table 3, is 18.6 cents if the retirement age is sixty-five. The tax is inversely related to the age of retirement, with the cost per worker being almost two and a half times as great when the retirement age is sixty as it would be if the retirement age were seventy.

---

[2] Robert Clark and John Menefee, "Federal Expenditures for the Elderly: Past and Future," *The Gerontologist*, forthcoming.

4

TABLE 3

Effect of Alternative Retirement Ages on Tax per Worker, 1978

	Retirement Age					
	55	60	62	65	68	70
Labor Force (millions)[a]	108.4	119.6	123.4	129.0	134.3	137.6
Retirees (millions)[b]	44.7	33.5	29.6	24.1	18.8	15.5
Tax per worker per dollar of retirement benefit (cents)[c]	41.2	28.0	24.0	18.6	14.0	11.2

[a] The number of people between eighteen and the age of retirement.

[b] The number of people at or older than the age of retirement.

[c] The tax is calculated by dividing the number of retirees by the number of workers.

Source: Population data are for the civilian population in 1978 found in U.S. Bureau of the Census, "Estimates of the Population of the United States, by Age, Sex, and Race: 1976 to 1978," *Current Population Reports*, Series P-25, no. 800, (1979), table 3, pp. 15-16.

The effect of early retirement is illustrated further in the projections of future costs of providing benefits to the elderly. Table 4 indicates the future cost per worker relative to the 1978 tax rate (T) if the replacement ratio (the ratio of benefits to real earnings—B/W) is held constant and the population is assumed to approach zero population growth. If, for example, the retirement age is held constant at age sixty-five, the tax rate must increase by 62 percent by 2050. This estimate is only slightly less than the 64 percent rise in expenditures for OASI as a percentage of payroll estimated by the board of trustees of the Old-Age, Survivors, Disability and Health Insurance (OASDHI) trust funds.[3] The cost per worker is also vividly shown to be influenced by the retirement age, with the required tax being twice as great when the retirement age is sixty-two rather than seventy. Lower fertility and reduced mortality rates will further increase these cost increases.

These figures obviously overestimate the potential effects of changes in the age of eligibility for benefits in retirement programs. If the age of eligibility is lowered, not all of the newly eligible bene-

[3] Board of trustees, Federal Old-Age and Survivors Insurance and Disability Insurance Trust Funds, *1980 Annual Report* (June 1980), p. 48, and *1979 Annual Report* (June 1979), p. 57. The estimate is for the intermediate assumptions used in compiling the projections.

TABLE 4

TAX RATES WITH CONSTANT BENEFIT/EARNINGS RATIO AND REPLACEMENT LEVEL FERTILITY

Retire- ment Age	Year									
	1978	1985	1990	1995	2000	2005	2010	2015	2025	2050
55		2.09T	2.12T	2.11T	2.17T	2.34T	2.60T	2.94T	3.33T	3.33T
62		1.31T	1.35T	1.36T	1.32T	1.33T	1.43T	1.60T	2.05T	2.05T
65	T	1.02T	1.07T	1.10T	1.07T	1.04T	1.08T	1.22T	1.59T	1.62T
70		0.64T	0.67T	0.71T	0.72T	0.70T	0.73T	0.81T	1.04T	1.00T

NOTE: In this table, T represents the 1978 tax rate. Tax rates are generated by assuming that the labor force (L) is composed of the population between eighteen and the retirement age and that everyone over the retirement age has withdrawn from the labor force and is receiving the average retirement benefit (B). In a pay-as-you-go system, tax revenues from earnings (W) of labor force participants must equal total benefits paid, that is, $TWL = BR$. The necessary tax is found by $T = (B/W)(R/L)$ where R/L is the ratio of beneficiaries to workers and B/W approximates a replacement ratio for preretirement earnings. The projections are determined by employing population estimates from the Bureau of the Census, Series II, which assumes the future attainment of replacement level fertility, 2.1 births per woman. If the benefit/earnings ratio is constant over time, the tax rate rises in direct proportion to changes in the ratio of beneficiaries to workers. The effect of changes in the age structure of the population is shown across any row in the table. For example, population aging increases the tax rate from T in 1978 to $1.62T$ in 2050 holding the retirement age at sixty-five. This effect is more clearly illustrated if the 1978 tax rate is assumed to be 10 percent. In this case, the tax rate in 2050 will be 16.2 percent.

SOURCES: Population data are from U.S. Bureau of the Census, "Estimates of the Population of the United States, by Age, Sex, and Race: 1976 to 1978," *Current Population Reports*, Series P-25, no. 800 (1979), pp. 15-16; and U.S. Bureau of the Census, "Projection of the Population of the United States: 1977 to 2050," *Current Population Reports*, Series P-25, no. 704 (1977), tables 8 and 11.

ficiaries would withdraw from the labor force. Conversely, not all of those ineligible for benefits would remain in the labor force if the age of eligibility is raised.

Retirement Policy in an Aging Society

Population aging is reflected in an increase in the proportion of the population in the older age brackets. Projections based on current trends in mortality and fertility indicate that during the next half-century the older population will increase in size relative to the total population. This change in the age structure is due primarily to the sharp decline in the birthrate since the early 1960s. Aging of population increases the cost per worker of providing benefits to older

TABLE 5
Estimated Expenditures of OASDI as a Percentage of Payroll, Alternative Assumptions

| Calendar Year | Estimated Expenditures | | | | Scheduled Tax Rate |
| | Alternative II | | | Alternative III | |
	OASI	DI	Total	OASDI	
1980	9.48	1.39	10.87	10.89	10.16
1981	9.94	1.39	11.33	11.65	10.70
1982	9.97	1.35	11.32	11.86	10.80
1983	9.91	1.29	11.21	11.80	10.80
1984	9.86	1.26	11.11	11.84	10.80
1985	9.79	1.22	11.02	11.85	11.40
1990	9.39	1.13	10.52	11.74	12.40
1995	9.35	1.14	10.49	11.78	12.40
2000	9.08	1.29	10.37	11.69	12.40
2005	9.02	1.46	10.48	11.98	12.40
2010	9.75	1.62	11.36	13.32	12.40
2015	11.09	1.70	12.79	15.42	12.40
2020	12.82	1.73	14.55	18.13	12.40
2025	14.40	1.68	16.08	20.89	12.40
2030	15.37	1.60	16.98	23.22	12.40
2040	15.31	1.59	16.90	26.05	12.40
2050	15.33	1.63	16.96	28.80	12.40
2055	15.45	1.61	17.07	29.83	12.40

NOTE: These alternatives differ because of assumptions of trends in real GNP, wages, consumer price index, annual interest rate, unemployment rate, fertility rate, mortality rate, and the incidence of disability. The projections are based on the effects of current legislation.

SOURCE: Board of Trustees, Federal Old-Age and Survivors Insurance and Disability Insurance Trust Funds, *1980 Annual Report* (June 1980), pp. 48-49. For definitions of alternatives II and III, see pp. 21-28 of the report.

beneficiaries for any specified age of eligibility, as indicated by the projected rise in the percentage of covered earnings necessary to finance future social security benefits.[4] Table 5 shows that expenditures for OASI as a percentage of taxable payroll rise from 9.48 percent in 1980 to 15.45 percent in 2055, with the intermediate set of assumptions (alternative II) used by the board of trustees of the Federal Old-Age and Survivors Insurance and Disability Insurance

[4] Federal Old-Age and Survivors Insurance and Disability Insurance Trust Funds, *1980 Annual Report*, p. 48.

trust funds. If disability insurance is included, the increase is from 10.87 to 17.07 percent. Under a more pessimistic but perhaps more realistic set of assumptions (alternative III), expenditures reach 29.83 percent of taxable payroll. As a result, population aging is conducive to the formulation of new government policies to encourage delayed retirement.[5] One purpose of this study is to identify the role of current government policies in encouraging early retirement. Various programs and regulations that make early retirement an attractive alternative should be carefully scrutinized. Government should not compel older workers to remain in the labor force, nor should it subsidize early retirement. The pressure of rising costs due to population aging has stimulated a debate on public policies influencing retirement decisions. This study outlines some of the important issues for this debate.

[5] For an elaboration of this point, see Robert Clark and Joseph Spengler, "Economic Responses to Population Aging with Special Emphasis on Retirement Policy," in Robert Clark, ed., *Retirement Policy in an Aging Society* (Durham, N.C.: Duke University Press, 1980), pp. 156-66.

2

Increasing Propensity toward Early Retirement

Over the past century, workers in increasing numbers have ended their careers at age sixty-five or earlier and have withdrawn from the labor force. The tendency toward earlier retirement has accelerated in recent decades. This chapter examines the available evidence on the magnitude of this trend since the late 1940s; chapter 3 analyzes the determinants of these trends.

Retirement may be defined in various ways. An individual terminating a career is often said to be retiring from that job even though he may continue to work for another firm. Also, people may gradually retire when they shift from full-time to part-time employment. For some purposes, receipt of pension benefits is an appropriate indicator of retirement. The most comprehensive information available on retirement is data collected by the U.S. Department of Labor on labor force participation (LFP). LFP data by age and sex are available for 1900 to the present and are the principal measures of retirement employed in this study. Emphasis is placed on LFP because the total withdrawal from the labor force is apparently the primary method of reducing the amount of labor supplied. Table 6 shows that leaving the labor force was the option for reducing work time usually chosen by men in the Retirement History Study (RHS) between 1969 and 1971.[1] Of the white males in the study who were working in 1969, only 6.7 percent reduced their annual hours by more than 500 hours, whereas 30.6 percent left the labor force. This pattern con-

[1] The RHS is a national survey of individuals aged fifty-eight to sixty-three in 1969 conducted for the U.S. Social Security Administration. Persons were interviewed in 1969 and subsequently every two years until 1979. This survey is the data base for much of the new research by the authors cited in this report. For a more detailed description of the sample, see Lola Irelan, "Retirement History Study: Introduction," *Social Security Bulletin*, vol. 35, no. 11 (November 1972), pp. 3-8.

TABLE 6

CHANGES IN ANNUAL HOURS WORKED BY WHITE MALE WAGE EARNERS
AGED FIFTY-EIGHT TO SIXTY-THREE IN 1969

(percent)

Type of change	1971	1973
Hours of work increased by more than 500 hours since 1969	1.9	1.1
Hours of work did not change by more than 500 hours since 1969	60.7	32.4
Hours of work decreased by more than 500 hours since 1969 but worker remained in the labor force	6.7	9.3
Worker left the labor force	30.6	57.2
Total sample	100.0	100.0

NOTE: Columns do not add to totals because of rounding.
SOURCE: Retirement History Study, 1969, 1971, and 1973 surveys.

tinues through 1973. In addition, an analysis of the RHS data indicates that changes in LFP capture many of the changes in the other measures of retirement. For 93 percent of white male wage earners in the RHS, leaving the labor force was equivalent to being "completely retired," leaving their current job and "retiring," and adjusting hours worked by more than 1,000 hours. A factor analysis of indicators of retirement confirmed that these four labor supply measures are, for the most part, measuring the same event. For this reason, studies presented throughout the remainder of the chapter will treat these various definitions of retirement as if they were measuring the same event. By contrast, receipt of a public or private pension is apparently a different event from withdrawal from the labor force. In the RHS sample of white males in 1973, 6.3 percent were in the labor force and receiving a pension, whereas 24.6 percent were not in the labor force and were not receiving a public or a private pension.

Older Men in the Labor Force

Establishment of a Normal Retirement Age. The LFP rate of men aged sixty-five years and over has declined substantially since the late 1800s, and this trend has tended to establish sixty-five as the "normal retirement age" in the United States. There are two data sources illustrating the magnitude of this decline. Using census data, Clarence

Long reported that the LFP rate of men sixty-five and older declined from 71.3 percent in 1890 to 41.5 percent in 1940, or almost 6.0 percentage points per decade.[2] Table 7, based on data from the Department of Labor,[3] shows that this decline has continued during the past three decades, with the participation rate dropping from 45.8 percent in 1950 to 20.0 percent in 1979. Thus in thirty years the proportion of men sixty-five and over in the labor force has dropped from about one in two to one in five.

Another indicator of the extent of this decline is that despite a 23 percent increase in the population of males aged sixty-five and over between 1970 and 1979, there were 150,000 fewer men in this age group in the labor force in 1979. This decline has also accentuated the difference, with respect to participation in the labor force, between those younger than sixty-five and those sixty-five and older.

Early Retirement of Males. The LFP rate for men aged fifty-five to sixty-four historically has been above that of men over sixty-five. The rate for this group fluctuated about 94 percent between 1890 and 1930 before declining during the depression years and dropping to 88.7 percent in 1940. Table 8 illustrates that the proportion of men in this age group in the labor force remained about 87 percent during the 1950s. Since 1960 there has been a significant decline in the LFP rate of men aged fifty-five to sixty-four, a decline that increased in magnitude during the 1970s. The rate dropped from 83 percent in 1970 to 73 percent in 1979. This drop resulted in a work force of males aged fifty-five to sixty-four in 1979 that was approximately the same as in 1970, despite a 14 percent increase in the population. If the participation rate had remained at the 1970 level, there would have been over 975,000 more men of this age group in the labor force in 1979.

Men aged forty-five to fifty-four historically have been considered part of the prime-age labor force, and their participation rates have ranged between 95 to 98 percent. From the end of World War II until 1967, over 95 percent of males aged forty-five to fifty-four were in the labor force in each of the annual surveys. By 1979, however, the LFP rate of men in this age group had dropped to 91.1 percent. Table 9 indicates that this decline resulted in 365,000 fewer workers in this age group in 1979 than in 1970.

[2] Clarence Long, *The Labor Force under Changing Income and Employment* (Princeton, N.J.: Princeton University Press, 1958), p. 287.

[3] U.S. Department of Labor, *Employment and Training Report of the President* (1979).

TABLE 7

Civilian Population and Labor Force Sixty-five Years and Over
(in thousands)

Year	Total			Males			Females		
	Population[a]	Labor force	Percent	Population[a]	Labor force	Percent	Population[a]	Labor force	Percent
1950	11,378	3,038	26.7	5,358	2,454	45.8	6,021	584	9.7
1955	13,718	3,306	24.1	6,379	2,526	39.6	7,358	780	10.6
1960	15,356	3,194	20.8	6,909	2,287	33.1	8,398	907	10.8
1965	17,461	3,108	17.8	7,638	2,131	27.9	9,760	976	10.0
1970	18,947	3,221	17.0	8,075	2,164	26.8	10,887	1,056	9.7
1971	19,294	3,145	16.3	8,192	2,089	25.5	11,126	1,057	9.5
1972	19,917	3,107	15.6	8,287	2,022	24.4	11,667	1,085	9.3
1973	20,295	2,963	14.6	8,368	1,908	22.8	11,843	1,054	8.9
1974	20,709	2,920	14.1	8,594	1,925	22.4	12,146	996	8.2
1975	21,297	2,939	13.8	8,783	1,906	21.7	12,446	1,033	8.3
1976	21,772	2,874	13.2	8,946	1,816	20.3	12,902	1,058	8.2
1977	22,214	2,910	13.1	9,179	1,845	20.1	13,148	1,065	8.1
1978	22,701	3,042	13.4	9,380	1,923	20.5	13,333	1,120	8.4
1979	23,343	3,073	13.2	9,617	1,928	20.0	13,726	1,145	8.3

[a] Population figures are derived from data on the size of the labor force and the labor force participation rate for each year.

SOURCES: U.S. Department of Labor, *Employment and Training Report of the President* (1979), pp. 237–41; and unpublished data from the Department of Labor.

TABLE 8

Civilian Population and Labor Force Fifty-five to Sixty-four Years of Age

(in thousands)

Year	Total			Males			Females		
	Population[a]	Labor force	Percent	Population[a]	Labor force	Percent	Population[a]	Labor force	Percent
1950	13,462	7,633	56.7	6,667	5,794	86.9	6,811	1,839	27.0
1955	14,308	8,513	59.5	6,965	6,122	87.9	7,357	2,391	32.5
1960	15,412	9,386	60.9	7,373	6,400	86.8	8,027	2,986	37.2
1965	16,721	10,350	61.9	7,994	6,763	84.6	8,727	3,587	41.1
1970	18,248	11,277	61.8	8,583	7,124	83.0	9,658	4,153	43.0
1971	18,505	11,362	61.4	8,693	7,146	82.2	9,825	4,215	42.9
1972	18,903	11,361	60.1	8,867	7,138	80.5	10,033	4,224	42.1
1973	19,115	11,182	58.5	8,944	7,003	78.3	10,168	4,179	41.1
1974	19,288	11,187	58.0	9,083	7,030	77.4	10,214	4,157	40.7
1975	19,557	11,226	57.4	9,211	6,982	75.8	10,351	4,244	41.0
1976	19,857	11,279	56.8	9,357	6,971	74.5	10,482	4,308	41.1
1977	20,161	11,411	56.6	9,518	7,043	74.0	10,651	4,367	41.0
1978	20,415	11,555	56.6	9,642	7,087	73.5	10,792	4,468	41.4
1979	20,713	11,719	56.6	9,782	7,140	73.0	10,931	4,579	41.9

[a] Population figures are derived from data on the size of the labor force and the labor force participation rate for each year.

Sources: U.S. Department of Labor, *Employment and Training Report of the President* (1979), pp. 237–41; and unpublished data from the Department of Labor.

TABLE 9

Civilian Population and Labor Force Forty-five to Fifty-four Years of Age
(in thousands)

Year	Total Population[a]	Total Labor force	Total Percent	Males Population[a]	Males Labor force	Males Percent	Females Population[a]	Females Labor force	Females Percent
1950	17,235	11,444	66.4	8,473	8,117	95.8	8,778	3,327	37.9
1955	18,641	12,993	69.7	9,160	8,839	96.5	9,484	4,154	43.8
1960	20,599	14,852	72.1	10,004	9,574	95.7	10,598	5,278	49.8
1965	21,732	15,756	72.5	10,507	10,045	95.6	11,222	5,712	50.9
1970	23,060	16,949	73.5	11,058	10,417	94.2	12,006	6,531	54.4
1971	23,228	17,026	73.3	11,136	10,457	93.9	12,098	6,569	54.3
1972	23,343	16,970	72.7	11,182	10,422	93.2	12,148	6,548	53.9
1973	23,432	16,988	72.5	11,216	10,431	93.0	12,209	6,556	53.7
1974	23,572	17,137	72.7	11,335	10,451	92.2	12,245	6,686	54.6
1975	23,543	17,092	72.6	11,320	10,426	92.1	12,207	6,665	54.6
1976	23,404	16,991	72.6	11,269	10,322	91.6	12,125	6,669	55.0
1977	23,199	16,889	72.8	11,175	10,192	91.2	12,002	6,697	55.8
1978	22,966	16,903	73.6	11,086	10,122	91.3	11,876	6,781	57.1
1979	22,781	16,913	74.2	11,028	10,052	91.1	11,753	6,861	58.4

[a] Population figures are derived from data on the size of the labor force and the labor force participation rate for each year.

Sources: U.S. Department of Labor, *Employment and Training Report of the President* (1979), pp. 237–41; and unpublished data from the Department of Labor.

The LFP rate of men aged sixty-five and over has been falling for almost a century, but significant declines in the LFP of those aged fifty-five to sixty-four did not begin until the 1960s, and the drop in the work rate of men aged forty-five to fifty-four was a phenomenon of the 1970s.

Another indication of the trend toward early retirement is the proportion of eligible individuals aged sixty-two to sixty-four who opt for early social security benefits. Table 10 shows that the early acceptance rate rose for men from 34 percent in 1970 to 49 percent in 1976.

Older Women in the Labor Force

Changes in the labor force participation of older women differ considerably from the trends in participation for men forty-five and over. The LFP rate of females aged sixteen and over rose from 32.7 percent

TABLE 10

ELIGIBLE WORKERS AGED SIXTY-TWO TO SIXTY-FOUR
RECEIVING SOCIAL SECURITY BENEFITS
(percent)

Year	Men	Women	Total
1960	—[a]	44	44
1961	—	40	40
1962	20	41	28
1963	29	45	35
1964	31	46	37
1965	32	47	38
1970	34	46	39
1971	36	47	41
1972	39	49	43
1973	41	52	46
1974	44	54	48
1975	46	55	50
1976	49	56	52

NOTE: Workers entitled to disabled worker benefits are also insured for retired worker benefits and are included in those eligible for retired worker benefits. Therefore, disabled worker beneficiaries are also included in the number of eligible workers receiving benefits.

[a] Males were first eligible for early retirement benefits in 1962.

SOURCE: U.S. Social Security Administration, *Social Security Bulletin, Annual Statistical Supplement* (1975), p. 85.

15

in 1948 to 51.0 percent in 1979. Except for those over sixty-five, older women have participated in this movement toward increased market work. In the late 1950s, the LFP rate for females aged sixty-five and over rose to 10.8 percent, but it subsequently declined to about 8 percent in the mid-1970s. In 1979 there were approximately 1 million women sixty-five and over in the labor force (see table 7).

Between 1948 and 1970, the increase in the proportion of women aged fifty-five to sixty-four in the labor force exceeded the rise for all females. The participation rate of women in this age group rose from 27.0 percent in 1950 to 43.0 percent in 1970 (see table 8). This increase, along with population growth, raised the female labor force of this age group from 1.8 to 4.2 million workers during this period. After a slight decline in the early 1970s, this participation rate remained virtually constant during the five years from 1975 through 1979, whereas the participation rate for all women continued to rise.

A similar pattern of increasing participation for women aged forty-five to fifty-four is shown in table 9. The LFP rate rose from 37.9 percent in 1950 to 54.4 percent in 1970, while the total number of women in this age group in the labor force almost doubled. After 1970, there was a slight decrease in participation and then a subsequent increase to the 1979 rate of 58.4 percent. Thus, after two decades of sharp participation rate increases for women aged forty-five to sixty-four, only a moderate change occurred in the 1970s.

Early Retirement in the 1970s and 1980s

In the 1970s, there was an increasing tendency toward withdrawal from the labor force before age sixty-five on the part of men. For older women, the substantial increases in LFP registered from the 1940s through 1970 were significantly moderated in the 1970s. Table 11 shows that just under 1 million fewer people aged forty-five to sixty-four were in the labor force in 1979 than there would have been if the labor force participation rates of persons aged forty-five to sixty-four had remained at the 1970 level. Although actual numbers of people aged forty-five to sixty-four in the labor force rose from 28.2 to 28.6 million, the size of this group in 1979 would have been 29.6 million if the 1970 LFP rates had been applied to the 1979 population.

The size of the future labor force will depend on whether these current trends continue. Periodically, the Bureau of Labor Statistics (BLS) prepares labor force projections based primarily on past trends. As a starting point for the discussion of the possibility of reversing

16

TABLE 11

POTENTIAL AND ACTUAL LABOR FORCE AMONG PERSONS AGED
FORTY-FIVE TO SIXTY-FOUR, 1979

(in thousands)

Demographic Group	Labor Force 1970	Actual Labor Force 1979	Potential Labor Force 1979	Actual Minus Potential
Men (45–64)	17,541	17,192	18,507	−1,315
Women (45–64)	10,684	11,440	11,094	346
Total	28,225	28,632	29,601	−969

a The potential labor force equals the 1970 participation rate applied to the 1979 population.

SOURCE: Authors.

the trend toward early retirement, the 1978 BLS projections of the labor force until 1990 are briefly reviewed.

The first step in projecting the size of the future labor force is to estimate the size and age composition of the population. The BLS labor force projections are based on population estimates by the Census Bureau. Unexpected swings in fertility may be caused by fluctuating economic conditions, changing social values, wars, and changes in birth control technology. The size of a nation's population also depends on mortality and immigration rates. Because everyone who will be over sixteen years of age in 1990 has already been born, the size of the 1990 population of working age will be determined by future mortality and immigation rates.

The projections of the labor force participation rates in the 1980s made by the BLS are shown in table 12. The overall participation rate is expected to rise from 62.3 percent in 1977 to 66.2 percent in 1990, according to the intermediate assumptions. This increase is the result of a substantial rise in female participation, which is sufficient to offset a continued decline in the male participation rate. Virtually all of the decline for men is attributable to anticipated declines in participation of males aged fifty-five and over.

The participation rate of men aged fifty-five to sixty-four is projected to drop from 74 percent in 1977 to 65 percent in 1990 with the intermediate assumptions; with the high-growth estimates, the rate remains at 73.3 percent, but it drops to 59 percent if the low-growth estimates are employed. The participation rate of males aged sixty-five and over is expected to drop to 15 percent, with a range of between 9.4 and 18.1 percent. Despite the overall increase in the

TABLE 12

Civilian Labor Force Participation Rates, Intermediate Growth Assumptions

Demographic Groups	Actual Rates (percent)		Projected Rates (percent)	
	1970	1977	1985	1990
Total, age 16 and over	60.4	62.3	65.3(67.0–63.0)	66.2(69.7–63.0)
Men				
16 and over	79.7	77.7	77.0(79.4–74.7)	76.4(80.0–73.3)
16–24	69.4	74.1	76.4(78.9–74.4)	76.1(81.0–73.3)
25–54	95.8	94.2	93.5(95.1–92.2)	93.1(95.6–91.1)
55–64	83.0	74.0	68.1(73.5–64.1)	65.0(73.3–59.0)
65 and over	26.8	20.1	16.7(19.7–11.9)	15.0(18.1–9.4)
Women				
16 and over	43.3	48.4	54.8(57.1–52.4)	57.1(60.4–53.8)
16–24	51.3	59.6	69.8(73.2–66.2)	72.8(78.2–67.3)
25–54	50.1	58.4	68.5(70.9–65.9)	72.4(76.1–69.0)
55–64	43.0	41.0	40.2(41.5–38.1)	39.8(41.8–36.6)
65 and over	9.7	8.1	6.8(7.8–5.9)	6.2(7.2–4.8)

NOTE: Figures in parentheses indicate high and low assumptions.

SOURCE: Paul Flaim and Howard Fullerton, "Labor Force Projections to 1990: Three Possible Paths," *Monthly Labor Review*, vol. 101, no. 12 (December 1978), p. 28.

tendency of females to be in the labor force, the participation rate of females aged fifty-five and over is expected to decline slightly.

Applying the intermediate labor force participation rates to population projections produces an estimate of the size and composition of the labor force. Table 13 illustrates that the total labor force will increase to 119.4 million in 1990; however, the number of workers aged fifty-five and over is expected to decline. Despite an increase of 6 million in the poulation of males sixty-five and over, the male labor force for this age group will decline slightly from 1977 to 1990. The intermediate assumptions also predict that the labor force will have fewer males aged fifty-five to sixty-four and fewer females fifty-five and over in 1990 than at the end of the 1970s.

TABLE 13

Projected Growth of the Civilian Labor Force

Demographic Groups	Actual Labor Force (millions)		Projected Labor Force (millions)	
	1970	1977	1985	1990
Total, age 16 and over	82.7	97.4	113.0	119.4
Men				
16 and over	51.2	54.4	63.0	65.1
16–24	9.7	12.9	12.5	11.2
25–54	32.2	35.7	41.8	45.8
55–64	7.1	7.0	7.0	6.4
65 and over	2.2	1.8	1.8	1.7
Women				
16 and over	31.5	40.0	49.9	54.3
16–24	8.1	10.8	11.9	11.2
25–54	18.2	23.7	32.4	37.7
55–64	4.2	4.4	4.5	4.3
65 and over	1.1	1.1	1.0	1.0

Source: Paul Flaim and Howard Fullerton, "Labor Force Projections to 1990: Three Possible Paths," *Monthly Labor Review*, vol. 101, no. 12 (December 1978), p. 29.

If past trends continue as indicated by the BLS projections, the movement toward early retirement will continue. This will reduce the number of older workers and increase the number of retirees seeking public and private retirement and welfare benefits.

3

The Retirement Decision

The change in the labor force participation rates of persons aged forty-five and over during the past thirty years having been documented, speculation on the future course of retirement patterns requires an understanding of the factors that influence early retirement. This chapter outlines a theoretical model of lifetime labor supply that identifies the determinants of retirement. In addition, recent empirical research is reviewed to assess the importance of government policies, pension plans, economic conditions, and individual characteristics affecting the early retirement decision. Findings are analyzed in conjunction with changes in these factors during the past thirty years to identify the principal causes of the trend toward early retirement.

Model of Retirement Decisions

The retirement decision is one of the important job-related choices an individual encounters during his lifetime. The theoretical models developed by social scientists in recent years examine these labor supply decisions within a lifetime perspective.[1] Research based on these models indicates that individuals consider current and future opportunities in deciding how to allocate today's time and resources and in planning for the future. Of course, these plans may be altered by unanticipated events such as poor health or shifts in public policy.

[1] Alan S. Blinder and Yoram Weiss, "Human Capital and Labor Supply: A Synthesis," *Journal of Political Economy*, vol. 84 (June 1976), pp. 449-72; Gilbert R. Ghez and Gary S. Becker, *The Allocation of Time and Goods Over the Life Cycle* (New York: Columbia University Press, 1975); and James J. Heckman, "A Life-Cycle Model of Earnings, Learning, and Consumption," *Journal of Political Economy*, vol. 84 (August 1976, part 2), pp. 511-44.

In the labor supply model, the individual is viewed as making consumption and work decisions in response to his lifetime wealth, the value of time in the home and of time spent in market work throughout his life, preferences for consumer goods and services, and the desired timing of consumption. Increases in wealth reduce total lifetime labor supply and tend to induce earlier retirement. Examples of wealth gains would be unanticipated inheritances or changes in public policy that provide windfall gains to individuals. The development of social security and welfare programs probably fall into this category for people who retired in the 1950s and 1960s. Secular increases in real wages raise the lifetime wealth of successive cohorts and will likely contribute to reduce work time; however, wage changes also have substitution effects by altering the value of market work relative to time in the home.

Changes in the value of time in the home or at work may result in a reallocation of time. For example, as a result of the social security earnings test, individuals may spend more hours at work prior to receiving benefits and then reduce hours subsequent to receiving benefits, and they may retire earlier than they would have in the absence of the earnings test. Mandatory retirement policies and pension coverage will also affect the pattern of wages over the life cycle. The value of home time is affected by the presence of dependent parents or children. Health limitations will likely alter the value of time and will thereby lower personal wealth. The primary objective of empirical research is to estimate the effect of these variables on the labor supply decisions. This procedure necessitates an understanding of the complexities of pensions, social security, and economic conditions and of how these factors alter individual wealth and the value of time.[2]

Individual Aging and Retirement

In the life-cycle model, as people grow older they will begin to reduce their labor supply and will eventually withdraw from the the labor force. Individuals have diverse characteristics, preferences, and market opportunities, and this variation leads to retirement at different ages. As a group of individuals born during a particular

[2] For a comprehensive discussion of the existing evidence on the retirement of older persons, the reader is referred to Robert L. Clark, Juanita Kreps, and Joseph Spengler, "The Economics of Aging," *Journal of Economic Literature*, vol. 16 (September 1978), pp. 919-62. This study builds on the summary of Clark, Kreps, and Spengler on research completed since that time, and on new evidence from the Retirement History Study completed by the authors of this monograph.

TABLE 14

Labor Force Participation of Older Men, by Age, 1940 to 1979

(percent)

Age	Male Labor Force Participation Rate				
	1940	1950	1960	1970	1979
55	89.5	87.8	89.9	88.9	85.9
56	89.1	87.8	89.0	88.3	84.2
57	87.8	86.7	87.8	86.7	81.8
58	86.9	86.1	86.7	85.8	80.3
59	85.6	85.1	85.1	83.7	78.8
60	81.9	82.1	83.2	81.3	73.5
61	81.4	81.4	80.7	79.2	70.3
62	79.7	80.0	78.6	72.7	60.1
63	76.9	77.6	75.7	67.5	53.7
64	74.4	75.2	70.0	63.1	49.4
65	66.9	67.7	53.6	47.1	36.9
66	62.0	62.9	45.9	41.9	31.6
67	57.8	58.2	41.9	38.6	26.2
68	54.9	54.2	39.5	35.4	26.3
69	51.4	51.2	36.6	31.5	24.8
70	44.0	44.5	33.2	26.9	23.7
71	40.8	42.0	29.0	24.6	20.2
72	37.4	39.0	27.8	22.1	17.8
73	34.5	34.0	26.9	19.8	19.1
74	31.4	30.8	25.1	17.4	15.8
75 and over	18.2	18.7	15.6	12.1	8.7

Sources: U.S. Bureau of the Census, *Census of Population, 1970*, PC(2)-6A (1973), pp. 31-32; and unpublished data from the Department of Labor.

time period (such a group is often called a cohort) advances in age, more of the individuals in this cohort retire, and therefore the labor force participation rate of the group declines. Thus in a static environment the labor force participation rate of a cohort will decline with age.

This aging effect is difficult to determine from actual labor force data. For example, consider tables 14 and 15, which present single age LFP rates for census years 1940–1970 and for 1979. Reading down each column, we can see that the participation rate declines almost continuously with age. This decline, however, reflects both age effects and cohort effects, that is, differences due to different life experiences of individuals born in different years. Likewise, reading

TABLE 15

Labor Force Participation of Older Women, by Age, 1940 to 1979
(percent)

	Female Labor Force Participation Rate				
Age	1940	1950	1960	1970	1979
55	19.9	27.9	42.5	49.6	51.6
56	19.2	26.7	40.7	48.7	50.7
57	18.0	25.4	39.7	48.0	49.2
58	17.7	24.8	38.6	46.5	46.2
59	17.4	24.1	37.0	45.1	45.5
60	16.8	23.1	34.7	42.9	42.3
61	15.3	21.0	32.1	40.2	39.7
62	14.9	20.9	29.3	35.9	33.4
63	13.8	19.1	26.1	32.6	27.7
64	12.4	18.0	24.3	29.3	25.4
65	12.0	16.3	20.3	22.0	20.7
66	9.6	13.4	17.6	18.8	17.6
67	8.9	12.2	16.2	17.0	13.4
68	8.2	11.4	14.6	14.7	11.9
69	7.5	10.1	13.2	12.9	11.9
70	6.3	8.1	11.7	11.1	9.1
71	5.4	6.7	10.2	9.8	8.2
72	5.2	6.0	9.0	9.1	6.3
73	4.0	5.4	8.8	7.8	7.0
74	3.9	5.0	7.6	7.1	6.1
75 and over	2.3	2.6	4.3	4.7	2.7

Sources: U.S. Bureau of the Census, *Census of Population, 1970*, PC(2)-6A (1973), pp. 31-32; and unpublished data from the Department of Labor.

across a row in these tables confuses cohort effects with changes in wealth and economic incentives from one time period to another. With these caveats, it is interesting to note that the decline in LFP with age existed in 1940 for both men and women, before government and pension policies influencing labor supply became so widespread. In 1940, the greatest percentage point drop for males occurs between sixty-four and sixty-five years of age. Four decades later, participation rates still declined continuously with age. LFP rates are lower at every age, and the rate of decline with age has increased. In the 1970s, the two largest drops occur between sixty-one and sixty-two and between sixty-four and sixty-five. There is a similar age decline in participation by women.

The participation rates shown in tables 14 and 15 represent simple correlations between the incidence of being in the labor force and age. The pattern of LFP with age is clearly a function of numerous other factors; however, in econometric studies using cross-section data, the participation decline with age remains even after other determinants of labor supply are taken into account.[3] This finding illustrates the importance of the careful inclusion of an age variable in empirical studies of retirement, lest age effects be attributed to other characteristics that are correlated with age, for example health limitations and pension eligibility. If age is omitted from the labor supply equation but is highly correlated with health status and pension variables, then the influence of the "age effect" will be attributed to these other variables. Several of the most frequently cited studies of retirement have not included age as an explanatory variable, and this omission has probably biased their conclusions on the effects of health and pensions.[4] Using data from the Retirement History Study (RHS) on white males aged fifty-eight to sixty-three in 1969, labor force participation equations were estimated by the authors. Two primary results indicate that coefficient estimates are very sensitive to the omission of controls for age and that response to the independent variables varies with age.

Another significant finding from multiple regression studies is the large drop in the probability of labor force participation at age sixty-five even after controlling for pension eligibility and mandatory retirement. (See tables 14 and 15 for the simple age-participation relationship.) This effect may be due to conceptions of individuals and firms that sixty-five is the "normal" retirement age or to capturing a subtle aspect of the social security program or employer pensions not included in the empirical specifications (see subsequent sections in this chapter examining social security and private pensions).

The above discussion shows that age is an important predictor of the probability of an individual's being in the labor force and should be included as a control variable in cross-sectional analysis. Age itself, however, cannot explain the decline in the age-specific

[3] William G. Bowen and T. Aldrich Finegan, *The Economics of Labor Force Participation* (Princeton, N.J.: Princeton University Press, 1969); Robert Cotterman, "A Theoretical and Empirical Analysis of the Labor Supply of 'Older' Males" (Ph.D. diss., University of Chicago, 1978); and Herbert S. Parnes, *The Pre-retirement Years*, vol. 4, *A Longitudinal Study of Labor Market Experience of Men* (1975).

[4] Michael Boskin, "Social Security and the Retirement Decision," *Economic Inquiry*, vol. 15 (January 1977), pp. 1-25; and Joseph Quinn, "Microeconomic Determinants of Early Retirement: A Cross-sectional View of White Married Men," *Journal of Human Resources*, vol. 12 (summer 1977), pp. 329-46.

labor force participation rates since 1940. This decline over time, shown in tables 14 and 15, must be the result of changes in the determinants of each individual retirement decision. In the remainder of this chapter, these factors are examined with reference to their effects on LFP at specific points in time and their changes since the 1940s. It is useful to remember that secular declines in participation can be explained only by changes in the factors that influence retirement decisions. For example, health is an important factor governing current labor supply, but if the health status of older persons has remained constant or has improved, health will have no role as a cause of the trend toward early retirement.

Pension Characteristics

Social Security. The importance of the influence of the social security program on the retirement decision has been debated over a number of years with no final resolution of the issue.[5] Labor force participation may be affected by current eligibility for benefits, the amount of benefits, and how the system alters the gain from continued employment through the earnings test and the recomputation of future benefits.

Before examining each of these potential effects, it is necessary to outline briefly the major characteristics of the social security system.[6] The social security benefit formula has been altered periodically, but the basic structure has remained essentially the same. The average monthly earnings (AME) of an individual are derived from a person's past earnings history for earnings up to the maximum taxable amount after 1950 and before the year of retirement. Past earnings are now indexed to the growth in average wages up to age sixty. Years with the highest indexed earnings are used in computing the average, with the number of included years of earnings equal to the number of years between 1955 and the attainment of age sixty-two. After the average earnings amount is determined, a benefit

[5] See Colin D. Campbell and Rosemary G. Campbell, "Conflicting Views on the Effect of Old-age and Survivors Insurance on Retirement," *Economic Inquiry*, vol. 14 (September 1976), pp. 369-88, for a summary of the earlier debate. See Alan S. Blinder, Roger H. Gordon, and Donald E. Wise, "Reconsidering the Work Disincentive Effects of Social Security" (unpublished paper, Princeton University, Princeton, N.J., May 1979), for a detailed explanation of new aspects of the debate.

[6] For details of the Old-Age, Survivors, Disability, and Health Insurance program, see U.S. Social Security Administration, *Social Security Bulletin, Annual Statistical Supplement* (1976), pp. 5-31; and *Social Security Handbook* (July 1978).

amount is calculated using a progressive benefit formula, so that benefits increase with the AME, but at a less-than-proportional rate. As a result, low-income workers may receive a higher return on taxes paid. The benefit amount also increases by 50 percent for dependent spouses and for each child under eighteen, up to a family maximum. The worker receives a full benefit if benefits begin at age sixty-five; reduced benefits, however, can be taken as early as age sixty-two. If benefits start prior to age sixty-five, the size of the benefit is reduced by 5/9 of 1 percent for each month between the retirement age and age sixty-five. Similarly, if a person postpones receipt of social security benefits past age sixty-five, then benefits are increased by 1/12 of 1 percent per month. This delayed retirement credit will rise to 1/4 of 1 percent per month starting in 1982.

Within the framework of a life-cycle model, a mandatory program reallocating income from early in life to the older ages will not necessarily alter the pattern of labor supply. For example, in an actuarially fair social security system, the expected discounted value of retirement benefits (social security wealth) at the age of eligibility would be just equal to the total taxes plus interest that the worker has paid. In addition, the change in social security wealth from continued employment would be equal to the value of new taxes paid, and social security wealth would be unaffected by the timing of benefit acceptance. As a result lifetime wealth and the value of market time would be unchanged. Hence, labor supply would be unaffected by the program as long as the individual can borrow against future benefits at the same interest rate being used to determine the wealth value of social security benefits.

Actual market conditions and social security characteristics deviate from the system just described. First, individuals typically face a higher borrowing rate than the lending rate in credit markets, and it may be quite difficult to borrow against future social security benefits. Thus current eligibility for benefits might directly affect the retirement decision as individuals have access to the monthly flow of income. Unfortunately, most empirical studies have been unable to estimate a separate eligibility effect while holding other social security characteristics constant. If eligibility for benefits is the only social security variable in a labor supply equation, the estimated effect will include the response to the level of benefits and the earnings test, as well as the availability of benefits. Clark, Johnson, and McDermed find that after controlling for social security wealth, current eligibility continues to have a significant effect in inducing retirement. Quinn also presents evidence of a social security eligibility effect on men from the Retirement History Study. Lacking benefit data, Quinn uses current eligibility to capture the effects of the social security program. Quinn found a larger effect than Clark, Johnson, and McDermed, but he acknowledges that the social security effect may be biased, since age was not explicitly controlled for; instead, the eligibility-for-social-security variable was set equal to zero for those less than age sixty-two.[7]

This indicates that policy changes altering the age of eligibility will influence retirement decisions even if the discounted value of the flow of benefits is held constant. Thus lowering the age of first eligibility for benefits from sixty-five to sixty-two in 1962 for men probably encouraged a decline in the participation rate of men aged sixty-two to sixty-four during the 1960s. Conversely, increases in the age of eligibility, as recently proposed by a number of study groups, would tend to counteract the move toward early retirement.

The second potential effect relates to the size of benefits or social security wealth. In an actuarially fair system as described above, the size of retirement benefits will not alter individual labor supply. This conclusion follows from unchanged wealth and the ability to borrow against future benefits. The growth and development of the social security system has, however, raised benefits to all past and current beneficiaries beyond the level that could be financed from their own tax payments.[8] During the past three decades, coverage of the social security system has been extended from 64.5 percent of the total paid employment in 1950 to 90 percent in 1975. Changes in the benefit structure have produced higher benefits and an increase in the ratio of the average benefit received by a retired worker to average monthly earnings in the private sector. Table 16 shows the large increase in benefits and the ratio of average benefits to average earnings from 1950 to 1976. The expansion in coverage and liberalization of benefits has increased the benefits received by most individuals relative to the taxes they paid while still working. This increase in wealth has undoubtedly contributed to the trend toward early retirement.

[7] Robert Clark, Thomas Johnson, and Ann McDermed, "Allocation of Time by Married Couples Approaching Retirement," *Social Security Bulletin*, vol. 43, no. 4 (April 1980), pp. 3-17; and Quinn, "Microeconomic Determinants of Early Retirement."

[8] Joseph Pechman, Henry Aaron, and Michael Taussig, *Social Security: Perspectives for Reform* (Washington, D.C.: The Brookings Institution, 1968); and Donald Parsons and Douglas Munro, "Intergenerational Transfers in Social Security," in Michael Boskin, ed., *The Crisis in Social Security* (San Francisco: Institute for Contemporary Studies, 1977), pp. 65-86.

TABLE 16

Social Security Retirement Benefits and Private Sector Earnings

Year	Average Monthly Retired Worker Benefit	Average Monthly Earnings in the Private Sector[a]	Benefit as Percentage of Earnings
1950	$ 42.20	$230.05	18.3
1955	59.10	293.22	20.2
1960	69.90	349.30	20.0
1965	80.10	411.61	19.5
1970	114.20	517.26	22.1
1971	127.40	551.12	23.1
1972	157.10	589.57	26.6
1973	161.60	629.71	25.7
1974	183.10	668.77	27.4
1975	201.60	709.64	28.4
1976	218.80	763.34	28.7

[a] Weekly earnings were multiplied by 4.33 to convert to monthly earnings.
Sources: U.S. Department of Labor, *Employment and Training Report of the President* (1978), p. 266; and U.S. Social Security Administration, *Social Security Bulletin, Annual Statistical Supplement* (1976), p. 95.

Future retirees will not receive such windfall gains unless the social security system is further liberalized. Most individuals who spend their entire worklife covered by social security will receive relatively low rates of return from their payroll taxes.[9] Thus it would appear that within the framework of a stable social security system, the level of benefits or accumulated social security wealth will not be a major cause of continued early retirement. This is in sharp contrast to the past effects of program improvements that have played a major role in the early retirement decision.

Numerous empirical studies have attempted to estimate the effects of social security benefits on labor supply using cross-sectional data. In general, these estimates will be difficult to interpret and should not be thought of as showing the response of an individual to an exogenous increase in retirement benefits. Problems arise because the social security program provides greater relative benefits

[9] June O'Neill, "Returns to Social Security" (Paper presented to the annual meeting of the American Economic Association, Atlantic City, N.J., September 1976); and Dean Leimer, "Projected Rates of Return to Future Social Security Retirees under Alternative Benefit Structures," in *Policy Analysis*, Department of Health, Education, and Welfare Publication No. SSA 79-11808 (1978), pp. 235-68.

to low-wage workers than to high-wage workers, thereby increasing the lifetime wealth of low earners to a greater degree than high earners. As a result, low-wage workers should be more likely to retire earlier in the presence of social security than high-wage workers. In addition, high levels of social security benefits may reflect the labor market orientation of the worker rather than legislative changes in the level of benefits. These relationships will tend to produce a positive correlation between the size of social security benefits and labor force participation in cross-sectional data instead of the expected negative correlation that would follow from unexpected increases in benefits.

Empirical studies of retirement give some support to the argument that higher levels of social security benefits reduce labor force participation of persons over age sixty-five[10] but may not for those under age sixty-five. The results with respect to persons under sixty-five are not clear because of the previously noted econometric difficulties with using data on an individual's own benefits to determine to what extent social security induces early retirement.

The most frequently cited studies of the early retirement effect of social security benefits are those by Bowen and Finegan and by Boskin.[11] Both of these studies conclude that social security significantly reduces labor force participation; however, each suffers from problems that question the validity of this finding. The study by Bowen and Finegan has an inherent simultaneity problem because actual retirement benefits received are used rather than potential benefits. They acknowledge that this problem makes it unclear whether social security income caused retirement or retirement led to the receipt of social security income.

Boskin's study has a different problem of failing to control adequately for age. In his study, potential social security benefits are an important variable. Because of the actuarial reduction applied to benefits received prior to age sixty-five, once earnings are controlled for, younger persons will have lower benefits even if the wealth value of the lifetime flow of benefits is identical. With this formulation, the size of the social benefits will correlate highly with age.

More recent studies have used a social security wealth variable, which is formed by determining the present value of future expected

[10] For a summary of these findings, see Robert Clark and Joseph Spengler, *Economics of Individual and Population Aging* (Cambridge, England: Cambridge University Press, 1980), chap. 6.

[11] Bowen and Finegan, *Economics of Labor Force Participation*; and Boskin, "Social Security and the Retirement Decision."

benefits.[12] These studies, which directly incorporate age into the estimating equation, find that higher levels of social security wealth prior to age sixty-five are associated with either increased participation or had no effect. In summary, empirical research does not provide strong evidence that differences in social security benefits explain why some people retire early and others do not. Because of the econometric problems these estimates from cross-sectional data should not be used to measure the effect on the trend toward early retirement of legislative increases in the program. Unanticipated benefit improvements provide windfall gains to older individuals, which tend to reduce remaining lifetime labor supply.

The third labor supply effect of social security is the change in the net wage. The gain from continued employment is reduced by the payroll tax. In 1981, 6.65 percent of earnings up to $29,700 was paid by both the employer and the employee. In contrast to this tax, which is paid at all ages, the earnings test becomes effective only after the worker is eligible to receive benefits. If a worker aged sixty-five or over is currently receiving benefits, the earnings test reduces benefits by one dollar for every two dollars of earnings in excess of a minimum exempt amount, $5,500 in 1981. Beneficiaries estimate annual earnings, and benefits are withheld beginning in January until the expected level of reduction is attained. Errors in the estimation of earnings may be corrected throughout the year. The effect of the earnings test is that for many older workers the effective federal tax rate, including income and payroll taxes and the earnings test, will exceed 70 percent. Such a substantial marginal tax rate can be expected to reduce the labor supply of older workers.

Some have argued that the earnings test should not affect LFP because of the exempt earnings. The earnings test can influence labor force participation, however, despite the exemption of some earnings if firms offer lower wages for part-time work or if individuals incur significant commuting costs in getting to work. In the presence of these conditions, individuals may choose not to work at all rather than attempt to work for short hours. Another way of reducing earnings is to combine some weeks or months in full-time work with other periods of no work. This response would lower measured LFP.

[12] See, for example, David Barker and Robert Clark, "Mandatory Retirement and Labor Force Participation of Respondents in the Retirement History Study," *Social Security Bulletin*, vol. 43, no. 11 (November 1980), pp. 20-29; Cotterman, "A Theoretical and Empirical Analysis"; Laurence Kotlikoff, "Testing the Theory of Social Security and Life-Cycle Accumulation," *American Economic Review*, vol. 69 (June 1979), pp. 396-410; Clark, Johnson, and McDermed, "Allocation of Time."

Offsetting these tax effects are potential increases in future benefits because of continued earnings. Continued employment may alter the salary history used to determine the average monthly earnings, thereby raising future benefits. The AME is increased because a year of earnings in the 1980s may replace a year of earnings in the 1950s. Because the taxable maximum was low in the 1950s, earnings in later years will exceed those of earlier years for many workers. The gain in future benefits due to continued work is found by applying the benefit formula to the change in the AME. Through this effect, social security acts as a subsidy to continued employment, the value of which is a function of the worker's age, marital status, past earnings history, the appropriate discount rate, and current earnings. This effect is present throughout a person's worklife as he amasses quarters of social security coverage and builds an earnings history. After the worker has begun to receive benefits, this recalculation is done annually and may continue to increase future benefits.

In addition to the recalculation of benefits as a result of continued earnings, the monthly benefit amount is altered by the age of first acceptance of benefits. Between the ages of sixty-two and sixty-five, benefits are reduced by 5/9 of 1 percent per month if accepted prior to the sixty-fifth birthday; whereas deferment of benefits beyond age sixty-five increases the monthly benefit by 1/12 of 1 percent per month. This actuarial adjustment occurs in response to benefit acceptance rather than being determined by labor force status; thus deferment of benefit acceptance increases future benefits. Workers who have already started benefits may also receive a future recomputation of their benefits. At age sixty-five, monthly benefits are increased by 5/9 of 1 percent for every month prior to age sixty-five that monthly benefits were reduced due to the earnings test. This recomputation produces twelve points in the annual earnings pattern of individuals, where an additional hour of work raises earnings sufficiently so that the person has another month's benefits reduced due to the earnings test. In response to this first dollar of monthly benefit reduction, the beneficiary will receive a recomputation at age sixty-five.

It is the sum of these effects that determines whether the social security system penalizes continued work and encourages early retirement. The outcome is a function of the worker's age, marital status, past earnings history, the appropriate discount rate, and current earnings. Recent evidence indicates that recalculation of benefits and the actuarial increase in benefits may be sufficient to eliminate early

TABLE 17
Social Security Beneficiaries with Benefits Withheld

Year	Percentage with Benefits Withheld		Earnings Ceiling (1967 dollars)
	Age 62–64	Age 65–71	
1965	2.86	9.26	1,587
1966	2.77	16.82	1,543
1967	3.12	17.40	1,681
1968	2.95	17.38	1,613
1969	3.32	17.39	1,531
1970	3.06	16.35	1,445
1971	2.92	15.06	1,386
1972	2.68	13.65	1,342
1973	1.91	10.28	1,578
1974	1.64	8.35	1,625
1975	1.99	7.24	1,563
1976	1.76	6.64	1,619

Source: U.S. Social Security Administration, *Social Security Bulletin, Annual Statistical Supplement* (1965-1976).

retirement incentives for many workers, although some of the subsidy for continued work has been eliminated with the indexing of the wage history.[13] After age sixty-five, incentives to postpone receipt of benefits are not as strong, since benefits currently are increased by only 1/12 of 1 percent per month.

These effects suggest that relatively more people over sixty-five will be both beneficiaries and workers than in the population aged sixty-two to sixty-four. Table 17 compares the percentage of social security benefit recipients aged sixty-two to sixty-four who had benefits withheld and the percentage of those aged sixty-five to seventy-one who had benefits withheld. A much larger proportion of persons sixty-five and older worked and had earnings above the allowable maximum and therefore had benefits reduced. Because delayed retirement and acceptance of benefits after age sixty-five did not increase benefits at all prior to 1972 (and afterward by only a small amount), the earnings test seems to be a larger constraint on market

[13] For a debate on this point, see Richard Burkhauser, "An Asset Maximization Approach to Early Social Security Acceptance," Discussion Paper 463-77, Institute for Research on Poverty, University of Wisconsin-Madison, 1977; Blinder, Gordon, and Wise, "Reconsidering the Work Disincentive Effects of Social Security"; and Frank Sammartino, "The Timing of Social Security Acceptance by Older Men" (paper presented to the annual meeting of the American Economic Association in Denver, Colorado, September 1980).

work after age sixty-five than it does before age sixty-five. This is an expected result from a system that clearly is not actuarially fair after age sixty-five.

A second expected observation is that a number of people may work up to the maximum exempt earnings. This follows from the significant change in the net wage at the point where the earnings test becomes effective. Kotlikoff finds a bulge in the earnings distribution at this point that moves over time as the exempt earnings amount has been raised [14] (see table 18).

Few empirical studies have attempted to model all of these characteristics directly. Several studies have examined the effect of the earnings test on LFP and do provide some evidence that use of the earnings test tends to discourage work, especially after age sixty-five. Vroman found that the 1965 legislative amendments raising the earnings test ceiling on exempt earnings caused a small increase in the proportion of beneficiaries who had covered earnings. [15] On the other hand, Boskin finds the earnings test to be a large discouragement to work, stating that "the earnings test creates a huge distortion in the labor supply decisions of a large number of elderly workers." [16]

Employer Pensions. Private sector and government employee pensions are additional sources of lifetime wealth similar to social security benefits. A worker accumulates pension wealth throughout his work-life, and these benefits represent a reallocation of lifetime wealth. Coverage by an employer pension may increase lifetime wealth relative to private savings because of preferential tax treatment. In addition, the promise of pension benefits may alter personal and firm investment and employment decisions producing welfare gains. Finally, long-term employees under defined benefit plans implicitly receive wealth transfers from benefits that are not paid to workers that leave prior to vesting. Defined contribution plans typically approximate an actuarially fair system and would have little effect on lifetime wealth.

Pensions have several other aspects that may alter labor force participation. For example, receipt of monthly benefits is usually conditional on an employee's separation from the firm. This means

[14] Laurence Kotlikoff, "Social Security, Time to Reform," in Michael Boskin, ed., *Federal Tax Reform* (San Francisco: Institute for Contemporary Studies, 1978), pp. 139-42.

[15] Wayne Vroman, *Older Worker Earnings and 1965 Social Security Act Amendments*, U.S. Social Security Administration. Office of Research and Statistics, Research Report No. 38 (1971).

[16] Boskin, "Social Security and the Retirement Decision," p. 19.

TABLE 18

EARNINGS OF WORKERS SIXTY-FIVE TO SEVENTY-ONE, 1967–1974
(percent)

Earnings	1967 (Exempt Amt. $1,500)		1968–1972 (Exempt Amt. $1,680)		1973 (Exempt Amt. $2,100)		1974 (Exempt Amt. $2,400)	
	Men	Women	Men	Women	Men	Women	Men	Women
$ 1– 200	9.08	19.06	7.82	13.46	7.08	14.76	4.54	13.57
201– 400	6.12	11.44	4.84	9.89	5.09	8.28	3.81	10.00
401– 600	4.33	8.66	4.33	8.61	4.46	6.71	5.86	6.67
601– 800	4.86	5.03	4.19	4.56	4.06	8.28	4.39	7.14
801–1,000	4.75	7.28	4.66	5.18	3.41	3.80	4.10	5.71
1,001–1,200	6.02	5.89	4.94	6.09	3.80	6.49	4.68	3.81
1,201–1,400	5.07	5.89	4.00	4.23	4.59	4.25	1.76	2.14
1,401–1,600	11.51	9.18	7.15	5.98	5.24	6.04	4.25	3.81
1,601–1,800	1.90	0.35	7.62	6.35	4.85	3.58	4.39	1.90
1,801–2,000	2.01	2.60	2.27	2.30	6.03	6.26	5.56	4.76
2,001–2,200	1.06	1.91	1.43	2.19	7.60	6.26	3.95	6.19
2,201–2,400	1.69	0.87	1.02	1.53	2.62	1.79	9.96	5.24
2,401–2,600	0.42	1.04	1.02	1.68	0.92	1.34	1.90	2.38
2,601–2,800	0.74	0.35	0.90	1.39	0.65	1.34	1.46	0.71
2,801–3,000	2.32	3.47	1.51	1.60	1.31	1.12	2.78	0.71
3,001–3,200	0.42	1.21	0.82	1.35	0.26	1.12	1.46	1.19
3,201–3,400	0.42	0.52	0.65	0.98	1.31	1.12	0.29	1.19
3,401–3,600	1.37	1.91	0.90	1.09	0.79	0.45	1.17	0.95
3,601–3,800	1.06	0.35	0.84	1.09	0.52	0.22	0.44	0.71
3,801–4,000	2.32	2.25	1.31	1.20	0.92	0.45	1.02	1.43
Over $4,000	32.53	10.74	37.78	19.25	33.68	16.34	32.23	19.79
Total (%)	100.00	100.00	100.00	100.00	100.00	100.00	100.00	100.00
Sample size	947	577	4,895	2,741	763	447	683	420

SOURCE: Laurence Kotlikoff, "Social Security, Time to Reform," in Michael Boskin, ed., *Federal Tax Reform* (San Francisco: Institute for Contemporary Studies, 1978), p. 141.

that continued employment completely eliminates the pension bene-fit for that time period, creating an all-or-nothing form of an earnings test. Few plans, however, place restrictions on other market work; thus an individual can switch jobs and work full time in another job without loss of benefits from his original job. Large differences between the wage in one's career job and that associated with alter-native employment may lead to withdrawal from the labor force.

Pension benefits are similar to social security benefits in several ways. The size of the pension benefit depends on the wages of some portion of the worklife, usually including the final work year. Thus, continued employment typically raises future benefits. This recalculation effect is more important than for social security because there are usually fewer years in the averaging period and earnings are not indexed. In many plans, pension credits are not accumulated after the age of normal retirement.[17] By continuing to work, however, the individual forgoes current benefits. The net wealth effect from an additional year of work can be calculated, given the specific benefit formula. The gain in pension wealth is a function of the age of eligibility for full benefits and the reduction required for early retirement. Like social security, most pension plans will pay benefits prior to age sixty-five. In contrast, many employers offer early retirement with less than actuarial reduction in the size of the benefit, which provides incentives for early retirement.[18]

Clark and McDermed have shown that the net addition to compensation of pensions declines with age for most defined benefit formulas. This effect is a function of pension characteristics, inflation, and life expectancy. Under many circumstances, this effect will reduce the value of continued employment in a worker's early sixties and will therefore encourage early retirement. With high rates of inflation, this effect may lower compensation by as much as 10 percent.[19] Even if benefits are actuarially adjusted, pension eligibility, in the same manner as social security eligibility, may still have an effect if individuals face credit constraints and high transactions costs when they convert their durable assets to liquid assets. In this case, individuals might not consider the value of pension benefits until the age of eligibility (see the previous discussion on social security eligibility).

All research findings support the hypotheses that pension eligibility and higher levels of pension wealth lead to earlier retirement. Tabular data from the 1973 Retirement History Survey interview show for persons aged sixty-two to sixty-five a labor force participa-

[17] Lois Kopperman and Anna Rappaport, "Pension Welfare Benefits for Older Workers," *Aging and Work* (Spring 1980), pp. 75-87.

[18] Robert Frumkin and Donald Schmitt, "Pension Improvements since 1974 Reflect Inflation and New U.S. Law," *Monthly Labor Review* vol. 102, no. 4 (April 1979), pp. 32-37; and Alan Skolnik, "Private Pension Plans, 1950-1974," *Social Security Bulletin*, vol. 39 (June 1976), pp. 3-17.

[19] For a detailed discussion of these issues, see Robert L. Clark and Ann A. McDermed, "Inflation, Pension Benefits and Retirement," in *Retirement in the Dual Career Family*, U.S. Social Security Administration Grant No. 10-P-90543-4-02, Final Report (June 1980).

tion rate lower by eight percentage points for those covered by an employer.[20] Several additional studies using regression analysis have similar findings.[21]

Another group of studies using similar data but different specifications has found a much stronger effect of pension eligibility. Parnes estimates a twenty-percentage-point difference in retirement intentions before age sixty-five among workers eligible and those not eligible for pensions.[22] Barfield and Morgan, using a sample of auto workers, found a sixteen-percentage-point increase in the retirement rate once pension income exceeded $2,000 per year.[23] Similarly, Clark, Johnson, and McDermed, using a simultaneous family decision model, estimated that a husband's eligibility for a pension reduces his probability of labor force participation by over fifteen percentage points.[24] Finally, estimates from work by the authors of this report find the effects of eligibility in the same range for ages less than sixty-five.

The effects of pension wealth are clouded by the same econometric problems as social security wealth. There is some limited evidence that reductions in labor market activity result from higher levels of benefits[25] and higher levels of pension wealth.[26] Thus pension plans may alter the lifetime wealth of workers and also the net gain from continued employment. Most evidence indicates that the current pension structure tends to encourage early retirement through both effects.

The development of the employer pension system has tended to reduce LFP over the past several decades. Table 19 shows the growth in the number of workers covered by private pensions, from almost 10 million in 1950 to 30 million workers in 1975. This growth has exceeded the increase in total employment, raising the number of

[20] Lenore E. Bixby, "Retirement Patterns in the United States: Research and Policy Interaction," *Social Security Bulletin*, vol. 39, no. 8 (August 1976), pp. 3-19.

[21] Laurence Kotlikoff, "Testing the Theory of Social Security"; Quinn, "Microeconomic Determinants of Early Retirement"; Cordelia Reimers, "The Timing of Retirement of American Men," (Ph.D. diss., Columbia University, 1977).

[22] Parnes, *The Pre-retirement Years.*

[23] Richard E. Barfield and James N. Morgan, *Early Retirement: The Decision and the Experience* (Ann Arbor, Mich.: University of Michigan, 1969).

[24] Clark, Johnson, and McDermed, "Allocation of Time."

[25] Arden Hall and Terry R. Johnson, "The Determinants of Planned Retirement Age," *Industrial and Labor Relations Review*, vol. 33 (January 1980), pp. 241-54; and Barfield and Morgan, *Early Retirement.*

[26] The study of Clark, Johnson, and McDermed, "Allocation of Time," may provide a more precise estimate of the wealth effect by examining the coefficient on the pension wealth of one's spouse. They estimated that a $1,000 increase in pension wealth of one's spouse reduced participation by 0.2 percentage points.

TABLE 19

Private Pension and Social Security Coverage of Workers

Year	Private Plans		Social Security	
	Coverage (million)	Coverage as percentage of workers	Coverage (million)	Coverage as percentage of workers
1950	9.8	22.5	38.7	64.5
1955	14.2	29.6	55.0	85.3
1960	18.7	37.2	59.4	88.0
1965	21.8	39.5	65.6	89.1
1970	26.1	42.1	72.1	89.5
1971	26.4	42.6	72.9	89.4
1972	27.5	43.1	74.9	89.6
1973	29.2	43.7	77.3	90.0
1974	29.8	44.0	78.4	90.0
1975	30.3	46.2	77.6	90.0

Sources: Alan Skolnik, "Private Pension Plans, 1950-1974," *Social Security Bulletin*, vol. 39, no. 6 (June 1976), pp. 3-17; Martha Remy Yohalem, "Employee-Benefit Plans, 1975," *Social Security Bulletin*, vol. 40, no. 11 (November 1977), pp. 19-28; and U.S. Social Security Administration, *Social Security Bulletin, Annual Statistical Supplement* (1975), p. 68.

workers covered from 22 to 46 percent. During the same period, the number of beneficiaries rose from 450,000 in 1950 to over 7 million in 1975.[27] In light of the preceding discussion, expansion in coverage has contributed to the decline in labor force participation. Also, many firms have awarded prior-service credits to currently employed workers when they established a pension. Such windfall gains encourage reduced labor supply. During this period, employers also moved away from actuarial reductions for early retirement, lowered the normal retirement age, and in some cases shifted to the use of service requirements alone for the determination of benefit eligibility. All of these changes in pension characteristics generally tend to encourage early retirement.

Over the past several decades, the average monthly pension benefit has grown; however, the ratio of average private pension benefits to average earnings has remained relatively stable at approximately 25 percent. This indicates that benefits have been rising at the same rate as earnings. The lack of increase is in part

[27] Martha Remy Yohalem, "Employee-Benefit Plans, 1975," *Social Security Bulletin* (November 1977), p. 27.

illusory because workers have been leaving employment at earlier ages, thus reducing the level of benefits compared with average earnings. Also the expansion of pension coverage has meant that more lower-wage workers are now receiving benefits. The general conclusion is, therefore, that the development of employer pensions has encouraged early retirement.

Comparison of Social Security and Pension Effects. Employer pensions and social security provide income in retirement that is financed by taxes or contributions throughout one's worklife. These retirement income programs alter labor supply by changing the net compensation from continued work and through shifts in lifetime wealth. The following section summarizes and compares the retirement effects of the two systems. Both systems penalize continued work after eligibility for benefits. The social security earnings test disregards some levels of earnings and then reduces benefits one dollar for every two dollars of earnings until benefits are exhausted. Employer pensions typically pay no benefits if the person remains on the job but do not reduce benefits if the individual accepts another job. Thus the work penalty of employer pensions exceeds that of social security if the worker stays on the same job.

Delayed retirement may raise future benefits, as continued earnings raises the salary base, and benefits may not be reduced because of early retirement. In general, the change in average salary will be greater for defined benefit pensions than for social security because of the shorter averaging period (typically five years) and because covered earnings are not indexed as they are under social security. Therefore the gain from continued work through this effect will usually be greater for defined benefit pensions than for social security. Current law does not require that earnings and service after the normal retirement age be used toward the determination of pension benefits. Thus after the normal retirement age there may be no recomputation effect in many defined benefit plans.

The timing of benefit acceptance determines whether a beneficiary receives a full or reduced benefit. Sixty-five is the age of eligibility for unreduced social security benefits. Between sixty-two and sixty-five, benefits are lowered at approximately the actuarial rate necessary to keep the wealth value unchanged due to early retirement. Retirement after sixty-five raises benefits only slightly. Although sixty-five is frequently the age of eligibility for full benefits in employer pensions, an increasing number of plans make unreduced benefits available prior to sixty-five, and the penalties in defined benefit plans for early retirement have been reduced in recent years. In addition, no further increase in benefits is required after the normal retirement age. Pension characteristics vary from plan to plan; however, for many defined benefit plans the gain from continued employment through this effect is less than that for social security. In general, defined contribution plans will provide an actuarial increase in benefits for delayed pension acceptance.

This examination indicates that the early retirement incentives in employer pensions probably exceed those for social security. In addition, recent trends in pension characteristics have exacerbated the early retirement incentives.

Mandatory Retirement. Compulsory retirement is a personnel policy adopted by some firms that require workers to terminate their employment with that company at a specific age. It should be noted that mandatory retirement from one job does not force any worker to leave the labor force but is related to withdrawal from the labor force if a change results in loss of seniority and job-related skills that lower available wage offers. Data from the Retirement History Study indicate that most mandatorily retired workers do leave the labor force. For example, for white male wage earners aged sixty-six and sixty-seven who had reached mandatory retirement age, 12.4 percent changed jobs, 9.3 percent remained on the same job, and the remaining 78.3 percent left the labor force.

Mandatory retirement is closely related to pension plans. A 1961 survey of firms employing fifty or more workers indicated that very few of the plants with no pension plan have mandatory retirement clauses.[28] In the 1969 survey of newly entitled beneficiaries, four of five newly entitled beneficiaries with mandatory retirement on their most recent job were also covered by a pension. Data from the 1971 wave of the Retirement History Study paint a similar picture. Of those persons with pension coverage, 37 percent worked for firms without mandatory retirement, and only 18.6 percent of those whose companies had mandatory retirement provisions did not have pension coverage.

Cross-sectional and longitudinal studies estimate that mandatory retirement has reduced the LFP rate of males at age sixty-five by approximately five percentage points. Bowen and Finegan derive this figure from a comparison of participation rates of men aged sixty-four and sixty-seven.[29] Using coefficients from a cross-sectional study,

[28] Fred Slavick, *Compulsory and Flexible Retirement in the American Economy* (Ithaca, N.Y.: Cornell University Press, 1966).
[29] Bowen and Finegan, *Economics of Labor Force Participation.*

they assign five percentage points to that portion of the unexplained difference in time-series analysis of participation patterns attributed to compulsory retirement. Reno and Schulz find a similar effect from survey questions.[30] Barker and Clark, using cross-sectional and longitudinal data analysis, also find a five-percentage-point LFP decline among white male wage earners at age sixty-five.[31]

Theoretical and empirical research on the reasons for the existence of mandatory retirement indicate that it is part of an implicit long-term contract between the employee and the firm for which the employee receives increased compensation prior to mandatory retirement.[32] These models indicate that workers agree to lower wages early in their worklife in exchange for increased job security and the promise of higher wages if they remain with the company. This long-term contract creates incentives for both the employer and employee to invest more heavily in the worker's human capital. The fixed date of mandatory retirement terminates the contract at a time when wages are higher than they would have been without this implicit agreement. If so, the effect of compulsory retirement is to encourage retirement at age sixty-five but not earlier, as the increased compensation in higher wages or fringe benefits will encourage greater participation prior to age sixty-five. Some workers facing mandatory retirement, however, may leave their job prior to age sixty-five to seek other employment in anticipation of the compulsory retirement constraint; still, they may be unable to find suitable employment and so may leave the labor force. Evidence presented in Barker and Clark shows a small positive effect of mandatory retirement on labor force participation prior to age sixty-five.[33]

Health and Disability Income

Health Limitations. Health limitations affect the labor force participation of older workers directly by limiting their ability and desire to

[30] Virginia P. Reno, "Compulsory Retirement among Newly Entitled Workers," *Findings from the Survey of New Beneficiaries*, U.S. Social Security Administration, Office of Research and Statistics, Research Report No. 7 (March 1972); and James H. Schulz, *The Economics of Aging* (Belmont, Calif.: Wadsworth Publishing Co., 1980).

[31] Barker and Clark, "Mandatory Retirement and Labor Force Participation."

[32] Edward P. Lazear, "Why Is There Mandatory Retirement?" *Journal of Political Economy*, vol. 87 (December 1979), pp. 1261–84; and John Lapp, "An Economic Model of Mandatory Retirement," in *Outlawing Age Discrimination: Economic and Institutional Responses to the Elimination of Mandatory Retirement*, Administration on Aging Grant No. 90-A01738, Final Report (1979).

[33] Barker and Clark, "Mandatory Retirement and Labor Force Participation."

work and indirectly by reducing their productivity, which results in lower wage offers. The first effect clearly reduces labor force participation. The indirect wage effect has both wealth and substitution effects and theoretically has an ambiguous effect on labor force participation. Empirical research indicating that a lower wage tends to decrease the likelihood of being in the labor force is discussed later in this chapter. The decline in average health with age is one of the factors that produces the fall in labor force participation with age shown in tables 14 and 15.

A significant problem in empirically determining the magnitude of the impact of health on retirement is the lack of adequate objective health data in most national surveys. Self-perception of health may produce biased responses as the respondent attempts to give socially acceptable answers for labor force withdrawal.[34] Existing research studies have differed in the measure used to indicate health status and the point at which health status is determined. Despite the diversity of health indicators, virtually all studies of labor market activity of individuals fifty-five and over conclude that health limitations play an important role in the decision to withdraw from the labor force.

Although all studies find health to be important, there is debate about the magnitude of the effect. Part of the differences in previously estimated effects are due to the particular measure used and part are due to the point at which the measurement is taken. To test the sensitivity of the coefficient estimate to the particular definition of poor health, the authors estimated LFP equations using alternative measures of health status in the same specification with the same sample from the RHS. The coefficient estimates ranged from a low LFP decline of 20.7 percentage points for an objective measure, "unable to use public transportation" (with 11 percent of the sample having this limitation), to a 60-percentage-point change for those indicating that they have health limitations and are unable to work (with 21 percent of the sample having this limitation). The magnitude of the coefficient and the number of persons with health problems vary greatly.

A second difference across previous studies is the timing of the health measure. New estimates by the authors indicate that prospective health measurements have smaller coefficient estimates than concurrent or retrospective measures of health. Whereas the prospective measures find a zero- to ten-percentage-point increase in retirement

34 For a discussion of the influence of health on retirement and the problem of socially acceptable answer bias, see Campbell and Campbell, "Conflicting Views."

for those with a health problem, cross-sectional studies with con-current measures find differences of twenty to thirty percentage points. The differences can be reconciled if health changes occur as persons age, or the differences could be attributed to the fact that some respondents give "socially acceptable answers."

The importance of health in an individual's decision to retire is one of the most significant findings from cross-sectional research studies. Over time, however, the health of older persons has appar-ently been improving, and this should have encouraged later, not earlier, retirement. For example, the use of mortality or life expec-tancy as health measures indicates that the average health of older cohorts has improved during the last two decades.[35] Although medical innovations may have made it possible for persons in poor health to live to older ages, thus reducing the average health of a cohort, it seems highly unlikely that this could have a major depressing effect on the participation rate of this age group. On balance, health changes should not have exacerbated the trend toward early retirement and have probably tended to offset reductions that would otherwise have lowered participation rates even further.

Disability Income. Public and private disability programs provide income to individuals with health limitations. It is important to note that the relationship between health and disability income has not remained constant since 1956. During the past quarter of a century, disability insurance programs have increased in coverage and in the generosity of their benefits. In many cases, these benefits are conditional on the disability limiting work activity, with labor force participation being prima facie evidence that the health limitation is not sufficent to justify continuation in the program. As a result, the spread of disability programs has reduced work effort by individuals who might qualify for these benefits.

The largest of these programs is the social security disability insurance system (DI). This program was initiated in 1956 and was at first limited to disabled workers aged fifty and over. Since 1960, workers regardless of age have been eligible if they have had earnings in five of the ten years before they became disabled. Eligibility for these benefits creates an economic incentive for individuals to file disability claims and withdraw from the labor force.[36]

[35] Jacob Siegal, "Prospective Trends in the Size and Structure of the Elderly Population, Impact of Mortality Trends and Some Implications." *Current Population Reports, Special Studies,* Series P-23, no. 78 (1978), p. 23.

[36] Charles Meyer, *Social Security Disability Insurance* (Washington, D.C.: Amer-ican Enterprise Institute, 1979) provides a useful review of the development of disability insurance and some of its primary effects.

Studies by Gastwirth and Siskind estimate that the disability insurance program has lowered the labor force participation rate for males aged twenty-five to fifty-four.[37] Donald Parsons employs the older men's sample of the National Longitudinal Survey to estimate the effect of the level of disability benefits on labor force participation.[38] He estimates that there is a significant reduction in the participation rate with increases in the ratio of benefits to the wage rate. This result indicates that the level of transfer payments is a significant determinant of withdrawal from the labor force even if the program benefits are rigidly dependent on health status, a conclusion supported by the findings of Clark, Johnson, and McDermed where a $1,000 increase in total disability income reduced labor force participation by ten to thirty percentage points.[39]

The rise in the ratio of disabled worker benefits to spendable earnings has been threefold since 1960, a much larger increase than that for even social security retirement benefits (see table 20). Until 1975 the rise in relative benefits was accompanied by a proportional increase in persons' newly awarded benefits. The growth in DI recipients is also due to the maturing of the program, the spread of information about disability insurance, and amendments reducing the restrictiveness of eligibility criteria. This development of the disability insurance program since the mid-1950s has been one of the primary determinants of reduced labor force participation of men prior to age sixty-five.

Other Financial Variables

The wage of an individual is another potentially important factor in the retirement decision. In the context of the life cycle, the effect of wages on labor force participation is ambiguous for two reasons. First, although increasing wealth would cause wage increases to decrease the supply of labor, wage increases would also increase the supply of labor by inducing the substitution of wage income for the value of labor in the home. Magnitudes of the negative wealth effect and positive substitution effect vary, depending on when during an individual's lifetime a change in wage occurs. For larger wages over the entire lifetime, the wealth effect likely outweighs the substitution

[37] Joseph Gastwirth, "On the Decline of Male Labor Force Participation," *Monthly Labor Review,* vol. 95, no. 10 (October 1972), pp. 44–46; Frederick Siskind, "Labor Force Participation of Men, 25–54, by Race," *Monthly Labor Review,* vol. 98, no. 7 (July 1975) pp. 40–42.

[38] Donald Parsons, "The Decline in Male Labor Force Participation," *Journal of Political Economy,* vol. 88 (February 1980), pp. 117–34.

[39] Clark, Johnson, and McDermed, "Allocation of Time."

TABLE 20

NUMBER OF MONTHLY BENEFITS AWARDED TO DISABLED WORKERS ANNUALLY, 1957–1978

Year	New Awards	Ratio of Average Monthly Award to Average Spendable Earnings[a]
1957	178,802	0.070[b]
1960	207,805	0.141[b]
1965	253,499	0.270[c]
1967	301,359	0.255
1970	350,384	0.303
1971	415,897	0.312
1972	455,438	0.306
1973	491,616	0.350
1974	535,977	0.365
1975	592,049	0.374
1976	551,740	0.382
1977	569,035	0.388
1978	457,451	0.412

[a] Spendable earnings equal gross earnings minus social security payroll taxes and federal income taxes.

[b] Ratio is calculated from data presented in Parsons.

[c] Ratios for 1965-1978 are for the third quarter of each year as found in Lando, Coate, and Kraus.

SOURCES: Advisory Council on Social Security, *Social Security Financing and Benefits* (1970), p. 142; Mordechai Lando, Malcolm Coate, and Ruth Kraus, "Disability Benefit Applications and the Economy," *Social Security Bulletin*, vol. 42, no. 10 (October 1979), p. 8; and Donald Parsons, "The Decline in Male Labor Force Participation," *Journal of Political Economy*, vol. 88 (February 1980), p. 132.

effect, whereas wage increases just prior to retirement will increase participation as a result of a relatively larger substitution effect. Second, wage differences among older workers are due in large measure to previous decisions concerning investment in human capital. People who invested in relatively large amounts of human capital through more schooling or on-the-job training will have higher wages late in life and may have planned to retire later in order to capture the returns to this investment. In cross-sectional data, differences in individual wages are likely to be due largely to this latter effect rather than to differences in market opportunities.

In empirical studies, effects of wage changes on the probability of retirement vary greatly. Studies such as those by Parnes and Reimers that use the wage from a previous period find very small positive effects on labor force participation, effects that are not significantly different from zero.[40] Similarly, Quinn finds no relationship between wages and labor force participation using an imputed wage.[41] Boskin; Bowen and Finegan; and Clark, Johnson, and McDermed, on the other hand, do find a positive response of participation to higher wages.[42] The estimate from Clark, Johnson, and McDermed indicates a large (twenty-percentage-point) increase in participation with a one-dollar increase in the wage of married men.

The general increase in real wages since 1900, not captured by cross-section regressions, has increased lifetime wealth of each successive cohort leading to earlier retirement. Wage increases reflect productivity growth in response to greater use of physical capital, the long-term increase in investment in human capital, and technological change. Lewis argues that the rise in lifetime wealth from wage increases is one of the principal factors reducing lifetime labor supply.[43] Even before the advent of the social security system, labor force participation among older workers had been declining over a number of years partially as a result of this increase in lifetime wealth.

The increase in lifetime wealth should be reflected in increases in accumulated assets. A larger stock of wealth of an individual should unambiguously reduce lifetime labor supply. Still, the influence of asset holdings at older ages on a person's retirement decision is difficult to evaluate because asset holdings are endogenous and are determined simultaneously with life-cycle labor supply decisions. Kotlikoff has shown the dependence of savings upon retirement decisions using expected retirement age as a measure of retirement.[44] Thus empirical determination of the magnitude of the coefficient estimate of assets or asset income from a cross-section regression may be biased as such coefficient estimates are for social security and private pension wealth. In the few empirical studies that do not have serious

[40] Parnes, The Pre-retirement Years; and Reimers, "The Timing of Retirement."

[41] Quinn, "Microeconomic Determinants of Early Retirement."

[42] Boskin, "Social Security and the Retirement Decision"; Bowen and Finegan, Economics of Labor Force Participation; Clark, Johnson, and McDermed, "Allocation of Time."

[43] H. G. Lewis, "Individual Retirement Decisions: Discussion," in Robert L. Clark, ed., Retirement Policy in an Aging Society (Durham, N.C.: Duke University Press, 1980). Also see H. G. Lewis, "Hours of Work and Hours of Leisure," in Proceedings of the Ninth Annual Meeting of the Industrial Relations Research Association (1957), pp. 196–206.

[44] Kotlikoff, "Testing the Theory of Social Security."

measurement problems, larger assets or income from assets is associated with earlier retirement, though the effect is small.[45]

Economy Characteristics

Unemployment. The labor force participation rate of older males usually falls in response to short-run downturns in economic activity. This finding is supportive of the discouraged worker hypothesis, which states that after unsuccessfully searching for a job at acceptable wage rates, individuals withdraw from the labor force rather than continuing to search for employment. Older workers would be expected to be more sensitive to this effect because returns to search are lower (because of shorter work-time horizons), employment offers may be less frequent, and wage offers may be lower than previous wage offers that were dependent on firm-specific skills. In addition, pension income may be available to discouraged older workers.

For older persons, the departure from the labor force is more likely to be permanent than for younger individuals. Analysis of the RHS data indicates that the decision to retire from one's job for these persons tends to be an irreversible one. The problems of reentering the labor force are illustrated by the observation that for males who were out of the labor force in 1969, less than 20 percent reentered by 1973.

Clark, Kreps, and Spengler, reviewing time-series studies of the unemployment-participation relationship, conclude that an increase in the unemployment rate lowers the labor force participation rate among older workers. Bowen and Finegan find support for the discouraged worker effect using aggregate cross-sectional data. They estimate that a one-percentage-point increase in the unemployment rate is associated with a 1.2-percentage-point decrease in labor force participation for workers aged fifty-five to sixty-four. These studies have an econometric problem in that labor force appears in the denominator of both the dependent variable and an independent variable.

Further evidence for the higher unemployment/lower LFP rate relationship, however, is obtained from cross-sectional data on individuals. Several studies using an area or Standard Metropolitan Statistical Area (SMSA) unemployment rate variable confirm that higher unemployment causes lower labor force participation among

---

[45] Cotterman, "A Theoretical and Empirical Analysis"; Clark, Johnson, and McDermed, "Allocation of Time"; Quinn, "Microeconomic Determinants of Early Retirement"; and Reimers, "The Timing of Retirement."

the elderly, but the size of the effect varies somewhat across studies.[46] The implications of these findings are that recessions may permanently lower the labor force participation rates of older cohorts.

Inflation. Potentially, inflation affects older persons by raising the prices they pay and by changing their real income. Inflation may erode the value of wealth, though the effect is not as strong as one might suspect at first glance. The wealth of older workers consists of their homes, financial assets, private pensions, and social security benefits. Social security benefits are currently indexed by the Consumer Price Index, and this should prevent a decline in the real value of these benefits. Similarly, increases in housing prices have exceeded the inflation rate. Thus two of the major assets of many of the elderly have risen in real value. Other financial assets have not fared as well in the recent inflation, and this may have resulted in wealth losses for older persons. These are relative price changes within a general inflation, however, and the past trends may not be good predictors of future shifts in relative prices.

Employer pension benefits typically are not automatically adjusted for price increases. The promise of pension benefits is in nominal terms; thus inflation will lower the real value of these benefits as the retiree ages unless ad hoc increases are made by the employer. The loss of pension wealth through inflation can directly influence a worker's retirement decision and could delay withdrawal from the labor force. Continued employment enables older workers to receive the gain from higher wages and also to augment future pension benefits. The increase in the rate of inflation over the last decade has reduced the impact of pension wealth on labor force participation.

At present, no empirical studies have included an inflation variable explicitly in labor supply equations, but studies that have attempted to estimate the effects of wealth variables have been implicitly estimating the effects of inflation. The preceding review indicates that low-wage workers probably suffer lower losses in wealth because of inflation than do high-wage workers, since most of the assets of lower-wage workers are their home and social security benefits.

Demographic Variables

The migration of workers to urban areas and to jobs with less flexible working hours and conditions probably has contributed to the

---

[46] Reimers, "The Timing of Retirement"; and Quinn, "Microeconomic Determinants of Early Retirement."

decline in labor force participation among the elderly. Gallaway finds that states with higher degrees of urbanization have reduced rates of labor force participation among the aged.[47] Net migration to a city was found to decrease labor force participation of older men in the aggregate cross-sectional regressions of Bowen and Finegan.[48] A third study presents tabular data from the Survey of Newly Entitled Beneficiaries (SNEB) indicating that a higher percentage of urban than rural residents are retired (a nine-percentage-point difference).[49] The difference is attributed to the ability of rural residents to adjust their work hours in order to accept employment without losing social security benefits.

Much research currently is under way on the effects of different job structures that would allow more flexibility in working hours and job tasks. Theoretical models of life-cycle time allocation indicate that without constraints by firms on hours, workers would gradually reduce their hours of work rather than abruptly retiring. With flexible employment opportunities, workers are likely to remain longer in the labor force. Increases in employer hiring and training costs, however, may have reduced flexibility of working hours for some firms.

Demographic factors correspond to certain parameters of the life-cycle model but seem empirically to play a minor role in determining individual retirement patterns. Variables related to the number of dependents measure individuals' desires for wealth to purchase goods as opposed to their desires for time in the home. Race may also be an indicator of different preferences (not only with respect to goods and time, but also with respect to when consumption is desired) as well as of different market opportunities. Education perhaps indicates differences in the rate-of-time preference and also differences in the desirability of employment opportunities. Last, the spouse's market activities will likely have effects on retirement. If families with two workers make decisions jointly, the timing of retirement will be affected by the spouses' employment decisions.

Empirical studies show that married men retire slightly later than others, but there is not a consistent effect across studies. Similarly, although most studies are partitioned by race, those that have included

[47] Lowell E. Gallaway, *The Retirement Decision, an Exploratory Essay*, U.S. Social Security Administration, Office of Research and Statistics, Research Report No. 9 (1969).

[48] Bowen and Finegan, *Economics of Labor Force Participation*. There may be a problem of simultaneity in these estimates if labor market opportunities influence migration.

[49] Virginia Reno, "Why Men Stop Working before Age 65," in *Reaching Retirement Age*, U.S. Social Security Administration, Office of Research and Statistics Research Report No. 47 (1976), pp. 41–51.

48

race as an indicator variable find that black males retire slightly later than white males, though the effect is not statistically significant.[50] The number of dependent children increases participation by a small amount.[51] Having dependent parents, on the other hand, reduces labor force participation of males by a few percentage points.[52] Studies including variables related to the spouse find that spouse labor market activity increases the likelihood of an individual's remaining in the labor force, though higher wages may have a substitution effect.[53]

Factors Influencing the Labor Force Participation of Elderly Females

Retirement is less easily defined for women, since many women leave and reenter the labor force during their lifetime. The tendency in recent years for married women to become more established in the work force has led to new research interest in labor force participation among older women. Findings seem to indicate that women respond to the same incentives as males, but married women are more responsive than men to the level of family wealth and to their own wage and that of their husbands. Below are some important findings from Clark, Johnson, and McDermed for married women.[54]

Higher levels of asset income, home equity, spouse's social security wealth, and pension wealth lead to earlier retirement by married women. A woman's own social security wealth and pension eligibility do not decrease her participation in the labor force. The social security effect is similar to that for males, and it is assumed that the variables are proxies for career orientation and are merely reflecting past labor history. Past market experience is highly correlated with current labor force participation for these women.

Other important variables are own wage and spouse's wage. Women are two to three times as responsive as men to higher wages. A one-dollar increase in own wage increases participation by over fifty percentage points, whereas a similar increase in spouse's wage decreases participation by between fifteen and fifty-seven percentage

---

[50] Barfield and Morgan, *Early Retirement*; Parnes, *The Pre-retirement Years*; and Kotlikoff, "Testing the Theory of Social Security."

[51] Quinn, "Microeconomic Determinants of Early Retirement"; Parnes, *The Pre-retirement Years*; Barker and Clark, "Mandatory Retirement and Labor Force Participation."

[52] Barker and Clark, "Mandatory Retirement and Labor Force Participation."

[53] Boskin, "Social Security and the Retirement Decision"; Clark, Johnson, and McDermed, "Allocation of Time"; Cotterman, "A Theoretical and Empirical Analysis"; Reimers, "The Timing of Retirement."

[54] Clark, Johnson, and McDermed, "Allocation of Time."

points. Health problems, as measured by receipt of disability income, substantially reduce the probability of labor force participation. Also, the presence of dependent parents in the home is time-intensive and decreases participation of elderly married women. These findings are in general agreement with the earlier studies of Cain and of Bowen and Finegan that also indicate a strong negative correlation between the unemployment rate and the labor force participation of older women.[55]

For the future, then, there are two counteracting trends affecting female labor force participation. On the one hand, the longer period of labor force participation by women allows more investment in human capital, produces higher levels of wages, and tends to delay retirement. On the other hand, this longer continuous work period also results in eligibility for pensions and social security, producing higher levels of wealth and creating incentives for early retirement. In recent years, the wealth effect has probably increased in importance and may be responsible for stabilizing the participation rate of women between the ages of fifty-five and sixty-four in the 1970s.

Summary

Early retirement is induced primarily by the onset of poor health, the availability of retirement income from social security and employer pensions, pension characteristics that penalize continued work, the earnings test for social security, and unanticipated unemployment. These conclusions, based principally on cross-sectional studies, provide some insights into the determinants of the trend toward early retirement. The growth and development of social security and employer pensions have produced windfall gains in wealth for many older workers, thereby encouraging earlier retirement. Employer pensions increasingly have provided incentives for early retirement by penalizing continued employment.

The maturation and liberalization of the social security disability insurance program have created incentives for persons with health limitations to withdraw from the labor force and apply for disability income. Although the health of older persons as a group has probably improved in recent years, the interaction of health limitations and the availability of disability and other transfer income has likely intensified incentives for early retirement. Higher current wages encourage continued labor force participation of an individual; however, increases

[55] Glen G. Cain, *Married Women in the Labor Force* (Chicago: University of Chicago Press, 1966); and Bowen and Finegan, *Economics of Labor Force Participation.*

in the wage of their spouse lead to earlier retirement. By contrast, the long-term growth in real wages that has increased the lifetime wealth of successive cohorts has been a major factor in the decline of labor force participation. The retirement of wives is influenced by the same factors that govern the labor supply decisions of their husbands. Women appear to be more responsive to changes in their own and their husbands' wages. Current labor force participation of one's spouse encourages continued LFP; however, the long-term increase in female participation has likely contributed to the trend toward early retirement of married men. The next chapter highlights implications of the retirement process for the future based on our anticipated changes in the economic environment.

4

The Future of Retirement Patterns

Will the labor force participation rates of older persons continue to decline? The research findings examined in the preceding chapter identified health and the availability of disability benefits, employer pension benefits, rising standards of living, other economic conditions and personal characteristics as the principal factors governing individuals' withdrawal from the labor force before age sixty-five. In addition, initial eligibility for social security benefits and the existence of the earnings test also encourage workers to leave the labor force. Will future changes in these and other variables reverse the trend toward early retirement?

Health and Disability Benefits

In virtually all studies of labor market activity of individuals aged fifty-five and over, health limitations are found to be an important determinant of labor force participation. Yet during the past three decades, the health of older persons in the United States has probably improved. For example, mortality rates for the older age groups have declined, and life expectancy has increased. The effect of health, holding other factors constant, should have encouraged later retirement.

It is important to note, however, that the relationship between health and disability income has not remained constant since 1960. Of primary importance is the disability insurance program administered by the Social Security Administration that was enacted in 1956 and has subsequently been expanded and liberalized. During the period 1966–1975, the number of beneficiaries in the program rose from 1.9 million to 4.4 million, whereas total expenditures increased from $1.8 billion to $8.4 billion.[1] The average benefit increased from $101.20

[1] Mordechai Lando and Aaron Krute, "Disability Insurance: Program Issues and Research," *Social Security Bulletin*, vol. 39, no. 10 (October 1976), pp. 3–17.

in 1966 to $240 in 1975, an increase in real terms of 43 percent. The liberalization of disability benefits has been a major factor in the decline in labor force participation of men aged fifty-five to sixty-four between 1956 and 1976,[2] and also for younger men.[3] Increased enrollment rates could also be due to the spread of knowledge about the program and to reduced federal review procedures. The disability program should not have contributed directly to lower LFP rates for persons aged sixty-five and over because these individuals receive retired worker benefits. Indirectly, the reduction in the labor supply of younger persons will eventually lead to a reduction in the participation rate of older persons.

Looking to the future, the independent effect of health changes should be to encourage later retirement. Future effects of the disability insurance program are less certain. Growth due to the maturing of the program is probably past, and the program may also be affected by growing resistance to increases in all aspects of the social security program. Table 20 indicates that growth in this program has been reversed, as the number of new awards has fallen sharply since 1975. The Advisory Council on Social Security speculates that this is due in part to increased federal review of initial disability determination and to improving labor market conditions.[4] Further restrictions on eligibility and a lower rate of growth in real benefits will decrease the effect of this program on reducing the labor force participation rate.

Social Security Retirement Benefits

The research examined in the preceding chapter does not provide strong evidence that persons entitled to large social security benefits retire earlier than those entitled to relatively small benefits. Econometric problems may keep estimates from showing how an individual would respond to legislated increases in benefits. The actuarial reduction in benefits claimed before age sixty-five and the gain in benefits from continued work are probably sufficient to offset the earnings test—thus preventing the system from having a strong inducement for early retirement.

Table 16 shows that the average monthly social security retirement benefit rose from $69.90 in 1960 to $218.80 in 1976. This growth is attributable to higher wages of the more recent retirees and

[2] Donald Parsons, "The Decline in Male Labor Force Participation," *Journal of Political Economy*, vol. 88 (February 1980), p. 132.

[3] Frederick Siskind, "Labor Force Participation of Men, 25-54, by Race," *Monthly Labor Review*, vol. 98, no. 7 (July 1975), pp. 40-42.

[4] Advisory Council on Social Security, "Social Security Financing and Benefits," *Reports of the 1979 Advisory Council on Social Security*, p. 141.

TABLE 21

Cash Benefits from Old-Age and Survivors Insurance
(millions of dollars)

Year	OASI Benefits	Personal Income	Benefits as Percentage of Personal Income
1960	10,677	399,724	2.7
1965	16,737	537,031	3.1
1970	28,796	801,271	3.6
1971	33,413	859,092	3.9
1972	37,122	942,536	3.9
1973	45,741	1,052,440	4.3
1974	51,618	1,154,936	4.5
1975	58,509	1,253,367	4.7
1976	65,699	1,382,698	4.8

Source: U.S. Social Security Administration, *Social Security Bulletin, Annual Statistical Supplement* (1976), p. 94.

to periodic increases in the benefit structure. During the same period, average monthly earnings in the private sector rose from $349.30 to $763.34. As a result, the average monthly retired worker's benefit increased from 20 percent of monthly earnings in 1960 to 28.7 percent in 1976. Another measure of the relative rate of growth in retirement benefits is depicted in table 21, which shows that OASI benefits increased from 2.7 percent of personal income in 1960 to 4.8 percent in 1976. This increase was due to the growth in average retirement benefits as well as to the fact that increased numbers of people were eligible for benefits.

The growth and development of the social security system in the past two decades have created substantial wealth effects for older workers. These effects would be expected to have contributed to the trend toward early retirement. Further liberalization of the program is likely to be limited because the payroll tax rates necessary to finance the system are already very high and the current level of retirement benefits as compared to preretirement earnings approximates an acceptable relative level of retirement income for many workers.

Without the wealth effects of the past, the effects of social security on the tendency toward early retirement will be reduced. In fact, aging of the population will necessitate higher taxes, lower replacement ratios, or a later age of eligibility in the future that will cause a decline in lifetime wealth. An increase in the number of older persons eligible for retirement benefits relative to the number of people in the principal working ages is expected. Table 4 shows the effect of population aging on a pay-as-you-go retirement system. Holding age of eligibility and the replacement rate constant, there will be a substantial increase in the tax rate necessary to finance the system. (Also see table 5.) Clearly, increasing the age for benefits can significantly lower the necessary tax rate, as would a reduction in the replacement ratio. Each of these options would lower the lifetime return to social security coverage and would thus tend to discourage earlier retirement. Increasing the age of eligibility would probably have the greatest effect on the age of retirement. This observation is based on research findings of an eligibility and/or an age effect at sixty-five years, the current age of eligibility for full social security benefits. The policy change would be highly visible, would lower rates of return to the system, and would delay access to benefits. It would tend to delay retirement and substantially reduce the future tax rates required for social security.

Employer Pensions

Employer pensions alter the compensation to individuals from an additional year of work while promising a future stream of income. Eligibility for benefits and the value of these benefits have been identified as important determinants of retirement; however, only a few studies have been able to capture the effects of pension characteristics such as penalties for early retirement and the change in benefits from continued work on employment compensation. During the past three decades, pension coverage has grown more rapidly than total employment, increasing the proportion of the private work force covered by a pension from 22.5 percent in 1950 to 46.2 percent in 1975. Table 22 includes important data on the development of employer pensions. The expansion of coverage and the extension of prior-service credits to existing workers have contributed to the increase in early retirement.

The growth and expansion of the private pension system have apparently slowed in response to increased government regulation in the mid-1970s and the continuation of relatively high rates of inflation. Following the passage of the Employee Retirement Income Security Act (ERISA) in 1974, the rate of new plan adoptions slowed, and the incidence of plan terminations increased. There is some evidence that this may have been a temporary phenomenon as

TABLE 22

Pension Plans and Deferred Profit-sharing Plans of Wage and Salary Workers in Private Industry

Year	Coverage (millions)	Coverage as a Percentage of Workers	Employer and Employee Contributions (millions)	Contributions as a Percentage of National Payroll
1950	9.8	22.5	$ 2,080	1.67
1955	14.2	29.6	3,840	2.19
1960	18.7	37.2	5,490	2.46
1965	21.8	39.5	8,360	2.86
1970	26.1	42.1	14,000	3.25
1971	26.4	42.6	16,640	3.66
1972	27.5	43.1	18,540	3.74
1973	29.2	43.7	21,100	3.82
1974	29.8	44.0	25,020	4.14
1975	30.3	46.2	29,850	4.73

SOURCE: Martha Remy Yohalem, "Employee-Benefit Plans, 1975," *Social Security Bulletin*, vol. 40, no. 11 (November 1977), tables 1-4.

employers expedited terminations prior to full enforcement of the guidelines and deferred initiating new plans to observe the effect of legislation.[5]

The vesting and insurance provisions of ERISA increase the probability of a worker's receiving a retirement benefit if the worker has ever been employed by a company operating a plan; however, this legislation may have the unintended effect of reducing coverage in the economy. Continued development of the nation's employer pension system may have been slowed during the 1970s because of the prolonged period of relatively high unemployment and inflation. During periods of economic uncertainty, firms may be postponing compensation decisions whose costs will be determined by future economic conditions. In addition, unindexed pensions are less attractive to workers during periods of high inflation. Therefore, workers may prefer current compensation instead of a promise (in nominal terms) of future benefits.

[5] Pension Benefit Guaranty Corporation, *Analysis of Single Employer Defined Benefit Plan Terminations, 1976*, Publication No. PBGC505 (Washington, D.C., 1977).

Further expansion in pension coverage is also governed by the composition of the uncovered labor force. Presently, high-wage workers, union members, and employees in large companies are more likely to be participating in pension plans. High-wage workers have greater incentives to set aside current income for retirement saving, because they receive greater benefits from the nontaxation of employer contributions. Typically, they are better able to exert market pressure to achieve their desired form of compensation. Thus workers currently not covered by pension plans probably are less able and less willing to have current compensation lowered in order to finance contributions for a retirement plan. For these reasons it seems doubtful that the growth of pension coverage will continue at the same rate that it has during the past thirty years.

Without new government incentives or requirements, the rate of growth in pension coverage will slow, and further regulation such as reduced vesting or portability requirements could further retard the development of pension plans. Some analysts have argued that continuation of high rates of inflation and the inability of pensions to maintain real benefits will reduce workers' incentives to obtain coverage. The president's commission on pension policy has recently recommended that serious consideration be given to the establishment of a universal minimum advanced funded pension system.[6] Despite this recommendation, compulsory employer pensions in the private sector do not seem likely in the 1980s because of significant problems in the financing and coordination of pension credits across firms. In addition, the resulting reduction in current compensation may adversely affect the well-being of low-wage workers. Further incentives for the expansion of pension plans would probably produce income transfers to high-income workers. These income distribution effects of further subsidies to private pension plans will probably prevent the passage of major additional incentives to employers to initiate pension plans. Thus the spread of private pension coverage should not be a primary cause of any further reduction in the labor force participation of the elderly in the coming decade. Many employer pensions contain early retirement incentives, and recent changes in pension characteristics have incorporated greater financial incentives toward earlier retirement. For these reasons, participation in employer pensions will probably continue to encourage early retirement.

[6] President's Commission on Pension Policy, *An Interim Report* (May 1980), p. 10.

Mandatory Retirement

Earlier it was argued that the institution of mandatory retirement reduced the labor force participation rate of a cohort of men at age sixty-five by approximately five percentage points. The 1978 amendments to the Age Discrimination in Employment Act (ADEA) that preclude compulsory retirement prior to age seventy should tend to encourage delayed retirement. This and other policy changes may alter society's attitudes toward a "normal retirement age." Such a change should tend to reduce the age-sixty-five effect that many empirical studies have found. There is one potential perverse effect of the elimination of compulsory retirement on labor supply. If, as noted earlier, wages are higher in the immediate preretirement years due to implicit long-term labor contracts of which mandatory retirement is a part, the elimination of this policy may lower LFP prior to age sixty-five because of reduced compensation even as it increases labor supply after sixty-five.

In the past, firms and workers negotiated mandatory retirement provisions. The objectives and costs of this employment policy have not been clearly determined. One would suspect, however, that firms and individuals might now alter their behavior because of the prohibition of this type of contract. For example, some firms may attempt to adopt job retraining or redesigning. Others are likely to attempt to attain the previous age distribution of their work force by lowering wages or reducing the fringe benefits of their older workers. For example, benefits might be lowered by terminating pension credits at the normal retirement age, say sixty-five, or bonuses might be provided for early retirement. The response of firms to employees' desires for continued employment will be an important determinant of the final effect of outlawing mandatory retirement. Perhaps the most significant effect of this legislation is that in the long run it may make possible other policy changes that will encourage later retirement.

Economic Conditions

High rates of inflation can alter retirement decisions by changing the value of continued work and the level of real wealth of the individual. For older persons, the sensitivity of their potential retirement income to price changes has been moderated since the automatic cost-of-living adjustment for social security benefits was enacted in 1972. For most retirees, employer pension benefits remain quite vulnerable to the vicissitudes of inflation. The effect of inflation on real pension benefits affects the compensation from continued employment as well as pension wealth. The influence on other forms of wealth is less certain and depends on the relative price changes of the assets of the elderly. Based on limited current research, high rates of inflation should tend to encourage continued labor force participation through the effect on private pensions.[7]

During the past decade, the growth of productivity and real wages has slowed. The anticipated continuation of this trend will reduce the increase in lifetime wealth from one cohort to another. This trend was probably unexpected by workers now in their forties and fifties, and as a result these persons will have fewer accumulated assets than they anticipated. This loss in expected real wealth should tend to delay retirement. A continued slow rate of growth in real wages could be one of the most important factors leading to a reversal of the trend toward early retirement.[8]

Demographic Factors

Some researchers have argued that competition from younger workers created an economic and political environment that was conducive to early retirement.[9] Younger ages of retirement eligibility and reduced penalties for early retirement may have been the result of this demographic pressure. The relatively large influx of new entrants into the labor force that has characterized the past decade will not continue in the closing years of this century. Illustrative of this point is the observation that the ratio of persons eighteen to twenty-four to those aged eighteen to sixty-four declines from its 1976 level of 22.2 percent to 15.5 percent in 2000. This change in age composition will mean fewer young workers seeking to enter the labor force, and this should be conducive to delayed retirement.

---

[7] Robert L. Clark and Ann A. McDermed, "Inflation, Pension Benefits and Retirement," in *Retirement in the Dual Career Family*, U.S. Social Security Administration Grant No. 10-P-90543-4-02, Final Report (June 1980); and Robert Clark, "Impact of Inflation on the Aged" (paper presented to the annual meeting of the American Economic Association in Denver, Colorado, September 1980).

[8] For a review of the importance of the past growth in real earnings, see H. G. Lewis, "Individual Retirement Decisions: Discussion," in Robert L. Clark, ed., *Retirement Policy in an Aging Society* (Durham, N.C.: Duke University Press, 1980), and "Hours of Work and Hours of Leisure," in Proceedings of the Ninth Annual Meeting of the Industrial Relations Research Association (1957), pp. 196-206.

[9] Clarence Long, *The Labor Force under Changing Income and Employment* (Princeton, N.J.: Princeton University Press, 1958).

Since World War II there has been a significant increase in the tendency of married women to be in the labor force. During the next twenty years, many of these wives will be approaching retirement. To date, we know very little about the retirement decision of wives and how their increased labor force participation will influence the labor force withdrawal of their husbands. Available evidence indicates, however, that the increase in labor supply of wives early in life will encourage the earlier retirement of their husbands. Additional research is needed to examine family retirement decisions.

Higher levels of educational attainment frequently are associated with more pleasant job conditions, higher wages, and greater preferences for work. Better trained workers are typically in greater demand in the labor market and have less trouble finding and maintaining employment. The growth and development of education in the United States have meant that younger cohorts were more highly educated than their fathers and mothers. This difference in schooling created adverse employment prospects for older workers.

The recent decline in college enrollment rates combined with past investment decisions implies that the relative and absolute levels of schooling of successive older cohorts will not be as low in the future. Current projections indicate that the proportion of individuals fifty-five to sixty-four who are high school graduates will increase from 40 to 71 percent from 1970 to 2000, and for persons sixty-five to seventy-four, the graduation rate rises from 29 to 62 percent. Paralleling this rise is the increase in the ratio of average length of schooling for individuals sixty-five and over to persons twenty-five and over (from 73 percent to 94 percent by 1990). These changes in educational attainment should enhance the labor market status of the elderly and should tend to prolong their worklife.[10]

Conclusions

Labor force participation rates of males aged forty-five to sixty-four have declined steadily during the past two decades, whereas the decline in work rates of men aged sixty-five and over has continued throughout the twentieth century. Will this trend toward early retirement continue? Anticipated changes in most important determinants of retirement should tend to moderate the downward trend in the

[10] U.S. Bureau of the Census, "Educational Attainment," *Census of Population, 1970,* Subject Reports, Final Report PC(2)-5B (1973), table 1; U.S. Bureau of the Census, "Demographic Aspects of Aging and the Older Population in the United States," *Current Population Reports,* Special Studies, Series P-23, no. 59 (1976), p. 50.

labor supply of older men and, given likely shifts in public policy, may reverse the trend toward early retirement. Slowing economic growth and continued inflation should tend to encourage delayed retirement. Increases in life expectancy and other health improvements will influence workers to remain in the labor force. Population age structure changes also will be favorable to retaining older persons at work, as will future shifts in the relative degree of education of young and older persons.

Despite these changes that are favorable to continued employment, the reversal of the trend toward early withdrawal from the labor force probably depends on public policy decisions. Economic and demographic pressures will tend to prevent further liberalization in social security retirement and disability benefits. In fact, recent evidence suggests that modifications will be made in these programs that will encourage delayed retirement. The 1978 amendments to ADEA that preclude mandatory retirement prior to age seventy (and its likely total elimination in the near future), also will mean that more older workers remain in the labor force.

The effect of future pension regulation is more problematic. Laws governing the operation of pensions affect their coverage and may also alter many pension characteristics. Currently, federal regulations provide tax incentives for employer pensions and allow them to incorporate early retirement incentives. Shifts in government pension policies may have many complex effects, some of which may lead to new incentives for early retirement.

The continued aging of the population necessitates a careful reexamination of the nation's retirement policy. This report clearly indicates that current government programs are important contributors to the movement toward early retirement. Congress should act to eliminate government incentives for early retirement. The pattern of early retirement will depend in large measure on the actions of Congress during the 1980s. Most demographic and economic factors in the next decade will be favorable to later retirement, but reversal of the trend toward early retirement will probably await significant modifications in the national retirement policy.

5

Retirement Policy Reform

Population aging raises the tax on the working population necessary to finance a constant policy of retirement benefits. The continuing trend toward early retirement exacerbates these funding requirements. This study has indicated that the nation's retirement policies have contributed to early withdrawal from the labor force. The reversal of the trend toward early retirement may well depend on significant modifications in existing retirement programs. This chapter presents a policy agenda that would encourage continued labor force participation and would substantially reduce future taxes that support these programs.

Social Security Proposals

The projections of future costs for OASDI (see chapter 1) argue strongly for the immediate modification of the social security system. Any amendments that reduce the wealth value of social security benefits will tend to delay retirement, increase payroll revenues, and decrease total expenditures. Because of population aging, changes must be made in social security to maintain its pay-as-you-go financing. Either tax rates must be raised substantially, or lifetime benefits must be reduced. The most effective method of reducing social security wealth is to raise the age of eligibility for full benefits from sixty-five to sixty-eight, or even to age seventy. This increase should be done gradually, and people should be given the opportunity to plan for this change. Still, enabling legislation should be considered in the near future. For example, if age sixty-eight is the desired target, the increase in the age of eligibility from sixty-five to sixty-eight could be done over a twelve-year period, increasing the age of eligibility by three months each year. If such a program were to take effect in 1995, the retirement age would be sixty-eight in 2007, just at the time large future tax increases would otherwise be required. It would be advantageous to enact such a provision into law as soon as possible so as to enable individuals to adjust to this rather significant modification in the social security program. Increases in the age of eligibility for benefits are consistent with the improving health of older Americans and with their increasing life expectancy.

In principle the same reduction in social security wealth could be achieved by lowering future replacement ratios. This could be accomplished by altering the benefit formula or changing the indexing method of past earnings from wage to price indexing. The research findings examined in chapter 3 indicate that for similar reductions in social security wealth, increasing the age of eligibility will raise the labor force participation rate of older persons more than a lowering of replacement ratios.

Raising the age of eligibility is appealing because it simultaneously reduces benefit payments and increases tax revenues by encouraging continued employment. Within this framework, the earnings test for those over seventy should be abolished, but it should be retained for early retirees, with eligibility for reduced early benefits being raised to sixty-five. In this context, delayed retirement after age seventy should result in an increase in benefits that is actuarially fairer. Each of these changes would also increase the work incentives in the system by raising the gain from continued employment.

A potential effect of this policy is the likely increases in the number of persons applying for disability benefits. Although future improvements in health will moderate this effect, policymakers should recognize that some of the cost savings in payments to retired workers must be used to support increased disability expenditures.

Employer Pensions

Firms should not be required to provide pensions, and in most respects, further government regulation of employer pensions is not desirable; however, two issues merit serious consideration. First, careful examination should be conducted into the early retirement incentives of pension plans. The value of government subsidies through preferential tax treatment of pension systems that encourage early retirement should be reconsidered. The option of workers and firms negotiating such plans should not be prohibited, but there should be discussion of whether the government should change the relative costs to encourage the institution of early retirement incentives.

The second concept relates to the effect of inflation on the real value of pension benefits. The stream of pension benefits is essentially a lifetime investment that the retired worker is typically unable to alter through a shift in his investment portfolio. For defined benefit private pensions, the worker currently bears all the risk of price fluctuations, and firms receive all the potential gains from declines in the real pension liabilities. These gains may be shared with retirees through ad hoc increases in benefits. Despite this observation, firms should not be required to provide automatic cost-of-living adjustments to pension benefits, since this requirement would dramatically increase the cost of establishing an employer pension and would lead to the termination of many plans. Congress should, however, consider the possibility of selling indexed bonds to pension funds so as to provide some protection to retirees from the vicissitudes of inflation.

Summary

These policy changes, along with the trends described in chapter 4, should be sufficient to reverse the trend toward early retirement and should raise LFP rates of future older persons. Other policy amendments that could contribute to this reversal would be to raise the age of eligibility for other government cash and in-kind transfers and also the age for preferential tax treatment. Taken together, these shifts would reduce economic incentives for early retirement, dramatically lower government expenditures on older persons, and tend to stabilize the growth in tax rates necessary to support transfers to the elderly.